The Wicked Wit of
Charles
Dickens

The Wicked Wit

of

Charles Dickens

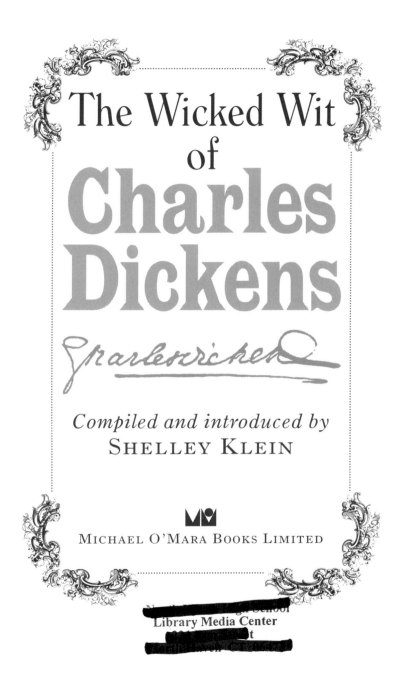

Compiled and introduced by
SHELLEY KLEIN

MICHAEL O'MARA BOOKS LIMITED

FIC
DIC

First published in Great Britain in 2002 by
Michael O'Mara Books Limited
9 Lion Yard, Tremadoc Road
London SW4 7NQ

A CIP catalogue record for this book is available
from the British Library

ISBN 1-85479-047-1

1 3 5 7 9 10 8 6 4 2

Designed and typeset by Martin Bristow

Printed and bound in Finland by WS Bookwell, Juva

Contents

Charles Dickens —

Introduction

B ORN at 387 Mile End Terrace, Landport, in Portsea, on 7 February 1812 (seven years after Nelson defeated Napoleon at the Battle of Trafalgar, and seven years before the birth of Queen Victoria), Charles Dickens was not only a child of the nineteenth century but also became one of its greatest social and political commentators. His early years were to all intents and purposes happy ones, for, as G. K. Chesterton wrote, 'He fell into the family . . . during one of its comfortable periods, and he never in those early days thought of himself as anything but as a comfortable middle-class child, the son of a comfortable middle-class man.' In fact, his father, John Dickens, was at the time of Charles's birth a clerk in the Naval Pay Office at Portsmouth, a job that obliged the family to move from naval port to naval port during the first ten years of the young Charles's life.

The second of eight children (six of whom survived) Charles was immediately recognized to be an exceptionally bright child (indeed some have surmised that he had a photographic memory). He enjoyed singing and performing and his father often took him to taverns where he would stand Charles on a table in order that he could perform. However, although family life was happy, it did have a dark side, for the fact was that Mr and Mrs Dickens had a penchant for living beyond their means.

When Charles was ten years old, the family moved once more, this time to London. The move to 16 Bayham Street, Camden Town – at that time nothing more than a dreary suburb – was coupled with a decrease in John Dickens's pay, which meant that the family now had a struggle to keep their heads above water. It was at this point that Charles received the first major shock of his life, for rather than being enrolled in school, he was instead expected to do odd jobs around the house and run errands.

Suddenly Charles's idyllic childhood was over – a fact that must have had a major effect upon the young Dickens – while the mounting debts that his parents were accruing (they had to sell the family furniture), no doubt added to his insecurity. At this point, Elizabeth Dickens tried to start up a small school, which she called 'Mrs Dickens's Establishment'. However, as Dickens later wrote, it was not a success: 'Nobody ever came to the school, nor do I recollect that anybody ever proposed to come, or that the least preparation was made to receive anybody . . .' Thus the school failed and Charles was found a job. James Lamert, a family friend, secured Charles a position at Warren's Blacking Warehouse, a shoe polish factory that stood at the edge of the River Thames at Hungerford Stairs. Aged twelve, earning six shillings a week, Charles's job was to paste labels on to the pots of shoe polish. The hours he worked were from 8 a.m. to 8 p.m. with a one-hour dinner break and a half-hour tea break. The job was both humiliating and tedious and the warehouse itself was a loathsome building, damp and overrun with rats. To make matters worse, on 24 February 1824, just a few days after he had started the job, Dickens's father was arrested and sent to the Marshalsea Debtors' Prison in Southwark.

In later years both these experiences, that of the blacking factory and of the Marshalsea Prison, provided Dickens

George Cruikshank

with a great deal of material on which to base his fiction (most notably *David Copperfield* and *Little Dorrit*), but at the time it can only be imagined how crushing and desperate these events were, not to mention how perilous it must have made life seem to the young boy. Dickens's mother and siblings accompanied his father and went to live inside the prison in one small room, while Charles was sent into lodgings beside the prison and continued to work at the blacking factory. It was a terrible time. Mrs Dickens tried to keep her family going by pawning what little jewellery she had left, and the odd piece of cutlery, while Charles trudged backwards and forwards between his lodgings and his work place. At night he read and re-read his old books – novels such as *Tom Jones* and *Robinson Crusoe*, wonderful adventure stories, which not only gave the young boy comfort, but also influenced him and gave him something to dream about.

It is estimated that Dickens spent a year working at Warren's until by a stroke of good fortune, John Dickens came into a small inheritance. On 26 April 1824 John Dickens's mother died, leaving him £450. This was not a lot of money even back then, but it was enough to clear his debts and, on John Dickens's release from the Marshalsea prison, the family returned to Camden Town and lodged temporarily with Charles's landlady. It was during this time that John Dickens decided that his son should leave the factory and be placed in a school. Charles's mother, on the other hand, was quite satisfied that her son should remain where he was and an argument ensued which, though won by his father, meant that Dickens never quite forgave his mother for wishing such a meagre life for her son. In *Great Expectations* Pip remarks: 'In the little world in which children have their existence whosoever brings them up, there is nothing so finely perceived and so finely felt as injustice.' It can only be surmised that Dickens was remembering the injustice meted out to him by his mother. One thing is certain, however – like Pip, Dickens now set himself to triumph over his circumstances through sheer hard work.

Dickens attended Wellington House Academy – a mediocre establishment, where he stayed for two years, after which he became a clerk at the law firm of Ellis & Blackmore in Gray's Inn. During this time Dickens also began to visit the theatre regularly and persuaded several

theatre managers to let him perform comic turns. Ever since he was a child and his father had set him up in taverns to sing and dance, it had been Dickens's wish to become an actor. Ironically he felt more himself when he was performing and his ability to mimic other people was legendary amongst his fellow workers. Dickens also thought, rightly or wrongly, that by becoming an actor he could leave, once and for all, the impoverished world he had come to inhabit and the meagre salary of a lawyer's clerk (approximately fifteen shillings per week), and establish himself with a modicum of wealth. Luckily for literature, Dickens's dreams of a life on the stage did not come to fruition. Instead, at the age of seventeen, he began scribbling down his observations on city life, on the people he met and came across in the street.

It was around this time that Dickens also determined to become a reporter for the political press and so enrolled on a shorthand course, which to everyone's amazement, he completed in just over three months (normally the course took three years to complete). Having learnt his trade he then went to work for *The Mirror of Parliament*. This was an exciting time to be a reporter. The Reform Bill was being made into law and there was a new Factory Act to control the number of hours that children should work, together with a new Poor Law. Charles threw himself into his job with gusto whilst at the same time contributing a series of stories to *Bell's Life in London* under the pen name 'Boz'. Then, at the age of twenty-three, Dickens was noticed by William Hall, a publisher with the company Chapman and Hall, who inquired whether he would be interested in writing a collection of stories about a group of Cockney sportsmen. The salary on offer was fourteen guineas a month.

This was a milestone in Dickens's writing career, for the collection would later become known as *The Pickwick Papers*, and following its success Dickens went on to write a serialization called *Oliver Twist* (1837–9), after which came *Nicholas Nickleby* (1838–9) and *The Old Curiosity Shop* (1840–1). All four of these novels, but in particular *Oliver Twist* and *Nicholas Nickleby* are vintage Dickens, displaying as they do, not only a social conscience, but also a concern for entertaining his audience. Indeed some of his most moving scenes are also some of his funniest and this

SKETCHES BY BOZ

George Cruikshank

flare for combining wit and wisdom was to become a trademark of all Dickens's best work.

Dickens was to publish fourteen major novels during his lifetime as well as numerous collections of short stories, plays and travel pieces, not to mention his many articles on social reform. He travelled, not only in Britain, but also to Europe and America, gave numerous readings of his work and vigorously campaigned on behalf of those less fortunate than himself. That his private life was no less frenetic is hardly surprising.

Having fallen in love and been rejected by a young woman called Maria Beadnell, Dickens went on in 1836 to marry Catherine Hogarth, the daughter of a fellow journalist, with whom he was to have ten children. It was during this marriage that Dickens wrote some of his most impressive work, namely *David Copperfield* (1849–50), which sold over 300,000 copies, *Bleak House* (1852–3), *Hard Times* (1854) and *Little Dorrit* (1855–7). Sadly however, Dickens's marriage was not to prove a happy one. Catherine was a shy, retiring woman who never really suited Dickens's outgoing temperament and, in 1858, much against Catherine's wishes, he separated from her and befriended a young actress called Ellen Ternan. There was at the time a great deal of conjecture about the nature of their relationship – whether she and Dickens were simply good friends, or whether they were lovers; and, indeed, speculations abounded as to whether or not she had given birth to Dickens's child (and if so whether or not that child had died) or had had an abortion. Whatever the case, Ellen Ternan became an important part of Dickens's life whereas Catherine did not, for, they separated and he went to live at Gad's Hill in Kent. It was here that he wrote *A Tale of Two Cities* (1859), *Great Expectations* (1860–61) and *Our Mutual Friend* (1863–4). However, by the mid-1860s

Dickens's health was failing (most likely due to his heavy work schedule) and his last novel, *Edwin Drood* was sadly never completed.

On 8 June 1870, after a long day's work, Dickens suffered a stroke and he died the following day. Public grief was universal. He was buried in the Poets' Corner of Westminster Abbey, where his grave was laid open for two days during which time countless mourners came to pay their last respects.

The death of Charles Dickens marked the passing of an entire period for, just as we view Victorian England through his novels and the marvellous stories and characters he created, so the Victorians saw themselves through the writing of their most beloved artist.

Definition of a Horse:
Childhood and
Adolescence

THAT FAMILY LIFE was at the centre of the Victorian social ideal and that the innocence of children was well-nigh sacrosanct is what the Victorians would have had themselves and others believe. However, the fact is that the Victorian period nurtured some of the poorest living and working conditions for both children and adults, in addition to which, family life was often far from pleasant. As if to make this point Dickens often populated his novels with highly dysfunctional families such as the Jellybys in *Bleak House* and the Gradgrinds in *Hard Times*, while several of his adult characters also testify to appalling experiences as waifs and strays having to fend for themselves. 'I've been locked up, as much as a silver tea-kettle . . .' says Magwitch in *Great Expectations*. 'I've been carted here and carted there, and put out of this town and put out of that town, and stuck in the stocks, and whipped and worried and drove. I've no more notion where I was born, than you have – if so much. I first become aware of myself, down in Essex, a-thieving turnips for my living. Summun had run away from me – a man – a tinker – and he'd took the fire with him, and left me wery cold.'

That Dickens suffered a similarly turbulent if not quite such a distressing time as a young boy is a matter of history and perhaps one that explains why the issue of childhood is so central to his work. But in addition to his fictional rampages, Dickens also tried to be more constructive when it came to the poor, in particular by lobbying for a better educational system. Knowledge, Dickens instinctively felt, was the only way to improve children's lives and, as he was to write in the *Examiner*, 'Side by side with Crime, Disease, and Misery in England, Ignorance is always brooding, and is always certain to be found.'

Of course, most children ended up in factories such as the one Dickens himself worked in – a memory that pursued the writer throughout adult life to the extent that he sought to reform the whole system. For instance, having visited a factory at the bequest of the Earl of Shaftesbury, Dickens wrote, 'So far as seeing goes, I have seen enough for my purpose, and what I have seen has disgusted me and astonished me beyond all measure. I mean to strike the heaviest blow in my power for these unfortunate creatures . . .'

Today, some hundred and fifty years or so later, that 'heaviest blow' endures in Dickens's characters like the Artful Dodger, David Copperfield, Smike and Oliver Twist – that he could also extract a certain degree of humour when describing them, and the terrible situations they found themselves in, only attests to his immense skill as a writer.

———◦◦◦◦———

Dombey sat in the corner of the darkened room in the great armchair by the bedside, and Son lay tucked up warm in a little basket bedstead, carefully disposed on a low settee immediately in front of the fire and close to it, as if his constitution were analogous to that of a muffin, and it was essential to toast him brown while he was very new.

Dombey and Son, 1846–8

✸

'Well,' said my aunt, 'this is his boy – his son. He would be as like his father as it's possible to be, if he was not so like his mother, too.'

David Copperfield, 1849–50

Much vexed by this reflection, Mr Squeers looked at the little boy to see whether he was doing anything he could beat him for. As he happened not to be doing anything at all, he merely boxed his ears, and told him not to do it again.

Nicholas Nickleby, 1838–9

❧

'. . . Give me your definition of a horse.'

(Sissy Jupe thrown into the greatest alarm by this demand.)

'Girl number twenty unable to define a horse!' said Mr Gradgrind, for the general behoof of all the little pitchers.

'Girl number twenty possessed of no facts, in reference to one of the commonest of animals! Some boy's definition of a horse. Bitzer, yours.'

The square finger, moving here and there, lighted suddenly on Bitzer, perhaps because he chanced to sit in the same ray of sunlight which, darting in at one of the bare windows of the intensely whitewashed room, irradiated Sissy . . .

'Bitzer,' said Thomas Gradgrind. 'Your definition of a horse.'

'Quadruped. Graminivorous. Forty teeth, namely, twenty-four grinders, four eye-teeth, and twelve incisive. Sheds coat in the spring; in marshy countries, sheds hoofs, too. Hoofs hard, but requiring to be shod with iron. Age known by marks in mouth.' Thus (and much more) Bitzer.

'Now girl number twenty,' said Mr Gradgrind. 'You know what a horse is.'

Hard Times, 1854

❖

The nephew revenges himself for this, by holding his breath and terrifying his kinswoman with the dread belief that he has made up his mind to burst. Regardless of whispers and shakes, he swells and becomes discoloured, and yet again swells and becomes discoloured, until the aunt can bear it no longer, but leads him out, with no visible neck, and with his eyes going before him like a prawn's.

'City of London Churches',
The Uncommercial Traveller, 1860

In the formal drawing-room of Stone Lodge, standing on the hearthrug, warming himself before the fire, Mr Bounderby delivered some observations to Mrs Gradgrind on the circumstance of its being his birthday. He stood before the fire, partly because it was a cool spring afternoon, though the sun shone; partly because the shade of Stone Lodge was always haunted by the ghost of damp mortar; partly because he thus took up a commanding position, from which to subdue Mrs Gradgrind.

'I hadn't a shoe to my foot. As to a stocking, I didn't know such a thing by name. I passed the day in a ditch, and the night in a pigsty. That's the way I spent my tenth birthday. Not that a ditch was new to me, for I was born in a ditch.'

Mrs Gradgrind, a little, thin, white, pink-eyed bundle of shawls, of surpassing feebleness, mental and bodily; who was always taking physic without any effect, and who, whenever she showed a symptom of coming to life, was invariably stunned by some weighty piece of fact tumbling on her; Mrs Gradgrind hoped it was a dry ditch?

'No! As wet as a sop. A foot of water in it,' said Mr Bounderby.

'Enough to give a baby cold,' Mrs Gradgrind considered.

'Cold? I was born with inflammation of the lungs, and of everything else, I believe, that was capable of inflammation,' returned Mr Bounderby. 'For years, ma'am, I was one of the most miserable little wretches ever seen. I was so sickly, that I was always moaning and groaning. I was so ragged and dirty, that you wouldn't have touched me with a pair of tongs.'

Mrs Gradgrind faintly looked at the tongs, as the most appropriate thing her imbecility could think of doing.

'How I fought through it, *I* don't know,' said Bounderby.

'I was determined, I suppose. I have been a determined character in later life, and I suppose I was then. Here I am, Mrs Gradgrind, anyhow, and nobody to thank for my being here, but myself.'

Mrs Gradgrind meekly and weakly hoped that his mother –

'*My* mother? Bolted, ma'am!' said Bounderby.

Mrs Gradgrind, stunned as usual, collapsed and gave it up.

'My mother left me to my grandmother,' said Bounderby; 'and, according to the best of my remembrance, my grandmother was the wickedest and the worst old woman that ever lived. If I got a little pair of shoes by any chance, she would take 'em off and sell 'em for drink. Why, I have known that grandmother of mine lie in her bed and drink her fourteen glasses of liquor before breakfast!'

Mrs Gradgrind, weakly smiling, and giving no other sign of vitality, looked (as she always did) like an indifferently executed transparency of a small female figure, without enough light behind it.

'She kept a chandler's shop,' pursued Bounderby, 'and kept me in an egg-box. That was the cot of *my* infancy; an old egg-box. As soon as I was big enough to run away, of course I ran away. Then I became a young vagabond; and instead of one old woman knocking me about and starving me, everybody of all ages knocked me about and starved me. They were right; they had no business to do anything else. I was a nuisance, an incumbrance, and a pest. I know that very well.'

His pride in having at any time of his life achieved such a great social distinction as to be a nuisance, an incumbrance, and a pest, was only to be satisfied by three sonorous repetitions of the boast.

Hard Times, 1854

'These, young ladies,' said Mrs Pardiggle, with great volu-
bility, after the first salutations, 'are my five boys. You
may have seen their names in a printed subscription list
(perhaps more than one), in the possession of our esteemed
friend Mr Jarndyce. Egbert, my eldest (twelve), is the boy
who sent out his pocket-money, to the amount of five-and-
threepence, to the Tockahoopo Indians. Oswald, my second (ten-and-a-half), is the child who contributed
two-and-ninepence to the Great National Smithers Testi-
monial. Francis, my third (nine), one-and-sixpence-half-
penny; Felix, my fourth (seven), eightpence to the
Superannuated Widows; Alfred, my youngest (five), has
voluntarily enrolled himself in the Infant Bonds of Joy,
and is pledged never, through life, to use tobacco in any
form.'

We had never seen such dissatisfied children. It was not
merely that they were weazened and shrivelled – though
they were certainly that too – but they looked absolutely
ferocious with discontent.

Bleak House, 1852–3

Some medical beast had revived tar-water in those days as
a fine medicine, and Mrs Joe always kept a supply of it in
the cupboard; having a belief in its virtues correspondent
to its nastiness. At the best of times, so much of this elixir
was administered to me as a choice restorative, that I was
conscious of going about, smelling like a new fence.

Pip, *Great Expectations*, 1860–1

It being a part of Mrs Pipchin's system not to encourage a child's mind to develop and expand itself like a young flower, but to open it by force like an oyster . . .

Dombey and Son, 1846–8

'. . . Now, here you see young David Copperfield, and the question I put to you is, what shall I do with him?'

'What shall you do with him?' said Mr Dick, feebly, scratching his head. 'Oh! do with him?'

'Yes,' said my aunt, with a grave look, and her forefinger held up. 'Come! I want some very sound advice.'

'Why, if I was you,' said Mr Dick, considering, and looking vacantly at me, 'I should – ' The contemplation of me seemed to inspire him with a sudden idea, and he added, briskly, 'I should wash him!'

'Janet,' said my aunt, turning round with a quiet triumph, which I did not then understand, 'Mr Dick sets us all right. Heat the bath!'

David, David Copperfield, 1849–50

'The twins no longer derive their sustenance from Nature's founts – in short,' said Mr Micawber, in one of his bursts of confidence, 'they are weaned . . .'

David Copperfield, 1849–50

I was always treated as if I had insisted on being born, in opposition to the dictates of reason, religion, and morality, and against the dissuading arguments of my best friends.

Pip, *Great Expectations*, 1860–1

❂

'We go upon the practical mode of teaching, Nickleby; the regular education system. C-l-e-a-n, clean, verb active, to make bright, to scour. W-i-n, win, d-e-r, der, winder, a casement. When the boy knows this out of book, he goes and does it. It's just the same principle as the use of globes. Where's the second boy?'

'Please, sir, he's weeding the garden,' replied a small voice.

'To be sure,' said Squeers, by no means disconcerted. 'So he is. B-o-t, bot, t-i-n, tin, bottin, n-e-y, ney, bottinney, noun substantive, a knowledge of plants. When he has learned that bottinney means a knowledge of plants, he goes and knows 'em. That's our system, Nickleby: what do you think of it?'

'It's a very useful one, at any rate,' answered Nicholas significantly.

'I believe you,' rejoined Squeers, not remarking the emphasis of his usher. 'Third boy, what's a horse?'

'A beast, sir,' replied the boy.

'So it is,' said Squeers. 'Ain't it, Nickleby?'

'I believe there is no doubt of that, sir,' answered Nicholas.

'Of course there isn't,' said Squeers. 'A horse is a quadruped, and quadruped's Latin for beast, as everybody that's gone through the grammar knows, or else where's the use of having grammars at all?'

'Where, indeed!' said Nicholas abstractedly.

'As you're perfect in that,' resumed Squeers, turning to the boy, 'go and look after *my* horse, and rub him down well, or I'll rub you down . . .'

Nicholas Nickleby, 1838–9

※

'Very well,' said this gentleman, briskly smiling, and folding his arms. 'That's a horse. Now, let me ask you girls and boys, Would you paper a room with representations of horses?'

After a pause, one half of the children cried in chorus, 'Yes, Sir!' Upon which the other half, seeing in the gentleman's face that Yes was wrong, cried out in chorus, 'No, Sir!' – as the custom is, in these examinations.

'Of course, No. Why wouldn't you?'

A pause. One corpulent slow boy, with a wheezy manner of breathing, ventured the answer, Because he wouldn't paper a room at all, but would paint it.

'You must paper it,' said the gentleman, rather warmly.

'You must paper it,' said Thomas Gradgrind, 'whether you like it or not. Don't tell us you wouldn't paper it. What do you mean, boy?'

'I'll explain to you, then,' said the gentleman, after another and a dismal pause, 'why you wouldn't paper a room with representations of horses. Do you ever see horses walking up and down the sides of rooms in reality – in fact? Do you?'

'Yes, Sir!' from one half. 'No, Sir!' from the other.

'Of course, No,' said the gentleman with an indignant look at the wrong half.

Hard Times, 1854

Droll, Droll, Very Droll: The Pickwick Papers

The Pickwick Papers was not Charles Dickens's first success as he had already published *Sketches by Boz* to good if somewhat limited acclaim. With *Pickwick*, however, he achieved both fame and fortune.

Having been approached by the publishing house of Chapman and Hall to write a series of stories about a group of men whose fishing and sporting exploits would see them in a series of comical situations, Dickens quickly set to work. The stories were to appear on a monthly basis in instalments of 12,000 words and although both the sales and reviews of the first few editions were disappointing, Chapman and Hall kept faith with their young author and, in time, *The Pickwick Papers* was a roaring success, selling over 40,000 copies of every edition. Indeed, the reviews for *Pickwick* were quite stupendous; one paper writing that 'Smollett never did anything better' while another compared Mr Pickwick and Sam Weller to Don Quixote and Sancho Panza – and this, no doubt, is where the popularity of the book lies, for, in creating characters like Sam Weller, Snodgrass and Mr Winkle, not to mention those truly awful newspaper editors Pott and Slurk, or the Parliamentary candidates Fizkin and Slumkey who spend most of their time hurling abuse at each other, Dickens had hit a rich seam of comic possibility and created a world in which, though tragedy existed, comedy prevailed. The following excerpt is but one such example . . .

———◦◦◦◦———

The more stairs Mr Pickwick went down, the more stairs there seemed to be to descend, and again and again, when Mr Pickwick got into some narrow passage, and began to congratulate himself on having gained the ground-floor, did another flight of stairs appear before his astonished eyes. At last he reached a stone hall, which he remembered to have seen when he entered the house. Passage after passage did he explore; room after room did he peep into; at length, as he was on the point of giving up the search in despair, he opened the door of the identical room in which he had spent the evening, and beheld his missing property on the table.

Mr Pickwick seized the watch in triumph, and proceeded to re-trace his steps to his bed-chamber. If his progress downward had been attended with difficulties and uncertainty, his journey back was infinitely more perplexing. Rows of doors, garnished with boots of every shape, make, and size, branched off in every possible direction. A dozen times did he softly turn the handle of some bed-room door which resembled his own, when a gruff cry from within of 'Who the devil's that?' or 'What do you want here?' caused him to steal away, on tiptoe, with a perfectly marvellous celerity. He was reduced to the verge of despair, when an open door attracted his attention. He peeped in. Right at last! There were the two beds, whose situation he perfectly remembered, and the fire still burning. His candle, not a long one when he first received it, had flickered away in the drafts of air through which he had passed, and sank into the socket as he closed the door after him. 'No matter,' said Mr Pickwick, 'I can undress myself just as well by the light of the fire.'

The bedsteads stood one on each side of the door; and on the inner side of each was a little path, terminating in a rush-bottomed chair, just wide enough to admit of a person's getting into, or out of bed, on that side, if he or she thought proper. Having carefully drawn the curtains of his bed on the outside, Mr Pickwick sat down on the rush-bottomed chair and leisurely divested himself of his shoes and gaiters. He then took off and folded up his coat, waistcoat, and neckcloth, and slowly drawing on his tasselled night-cap, secured it firmly on his head, by tying beneath his chin the strings which he always had attached to that article of dress. It was at this moment that the absurdity of his recent bewilderment struck upon his mind. Throwing himself back in the rush-bottomed chair, Mr Pickwick laughed to himself so heartily, that it would have been quite delightful to any man of well-constituted mind to have watched the smiles that expanded his amiable features as they shone forth from beneath the night-cap.

'It is the best idea,' said Mr Pickwick to himself, smiling till he almost cracked the night-cap strings: 'It is the best idea, my losing myself in this place, and wandering about those staircases, that I ever heard of. Droll, droll, very droll.' Here Mr Pickwick smiled again, a broader smile than before, and was about to continue the process of undressing, in the best possible humour, when he was suddenly stopped by a most unexpected interruption; to wit, the entrance into the room of some person with a candle, who, after locking the door, advanced to the dressing table, and set down the light upon it.

The smile that played on Mr Pickwick's features was instantaneously lost in a look of the most unbounded and wonder-stricken surprise. The person, whoever it was, had come in so suddenly and with so little noise, that Mr Pickwick had had no time to call out, or oppose their entrance. Who could it be? A robber? Some evil-minded person who had seen him come up-stairs with a handsome watch in his hand, perhaps. What was he to do!

The only way in which Mr Pickwick could catch a glimpse of his mysterious visitor with the least danger of being seen himself, was by creeping on to the bed, and peeping out from between the curtains on the opposite side. To this manoeuvre he accordingly resorted. Keeping the curtains carefully closed with his hand, so that nothing more of him could be seen than his face and night-cap, and putting on his spectacles, he mustered up courage, and looked out.

Mr Pickwick almost fainted with horror and dismay. Standing before the dressing-glass was a middle-aged lady, in yellow curl-papers, busily engaged in brushing what ladies call their 'back hair'. However the unconscious middle-aged lady came into that room, it was quite clear that she contemplated remaining there for the night; for she had brought a rushlight and shade with her, which, with praiseworthy precaution against fire, she had stationed in a basin on the floor, where it was glimmering away, like a gigantic lighthouse in a particularly small piece of water.

'Bless my soul,' thought Mr Pickwick, 'what a dreadful thing!'

'Hem!' said the lady; and in went Mr Pickwick's head with automaton-like rapidity.

'I never met with anything so awful as this,' thought poor Mr Pickwick, the cold perspiration starting in drops upon his night-cap. 'Never. This is fearful.'

It was quite impossible to resist the urgent desire to see what was going forward. So out went Mr Pickwick's head again. The prospect was worse than before. The middle-aged lady had finished arranging her hair; had carefully enveloped it in a muslin night-cap with a small plaited border; and was gazing pensively on the fire.

'This matter is growing alarming,' reasoned Mr Pickwick with himself. 'I can't allow things to go on in this way. By the self-possession of that lady it is clear to me that I must have come into the wrong room. If I call out she'll alarm the house; but if I remain here the consequences will be still more frightful.'

Mr Pickwick, it is quite unnecessary to say, was one of the most modest and delicate-minded of mortals. The very idea of exhibiting his night-cap to a lady overpowered him, but he had tied those confounded strings in a knot, and, do what he would, he couldn't get it off. The disclosure must be made. There was only one other way of doing it. He shrunk behind the curtains, and called out very loudly;

'Ha – hum!'

That the lady started at this unexpected sound was evident, by her falling up against the rushlight shade; that she persuaded herself it must have been the effect of imagination was equally clear, for when Mr Pickwick, under the impression that she had fainted away stone-dead from fright, ventured to peep out again, she was gazing pensively on the fire as before.

'Most extraordinary female this,' thought Mr Pickwick, popping in again. 'Ha – hum!'

These last sounds, so like those in which, as legends inform us, the ferocious giant Blunderbore was in the habit of expressing his opinion that it was time to lay the cloth, were too distinctly audible to be again mistaken for the workings of fancy.

'Gracious Heaven!' said the middle-aged lady, 'what's that?'

'It's – it's – only a gentleman, Ma'am,' said Mr Pickwick from behind the curtains.

'A gentleman!' said the lady with a terrific scream.

'It's all over!' thought Mr Pickwick.

'A strange man!' shrieked the lady. Another instant and the house would be alarmed. Her garments rustled as she rushed towards the door.

'Ma'am,' said Mr Pickwick, thrusting out his head, in the extremity of his desperation, 'Ma'am!'

Now, although Mr Pickwick was not actuated by any

definite object in putting out his head, it was instantaneously productive of a good effect. The lady, as we have already stated, was near the door. She must pass it, to reach the staircase, and she would most undoubtedly have done so by this time, had not the sudden apparition of Mr Pickwick's night-cap driven her back into the remotest corner of the apartment, where she stood staring wildly at Mr Pickwick, while Mr Pickwick in his turn stared wildly at her.

'Wretch,' said the lady, covering her eyes with her hands, 'what do you want here?'

'Nothing, Ma'am; nothing, whatever, Ma'am,' said Mr Pickwick earnestly.

'Nothing!' said the lady, looking up.

'Nothing, Ma'am, upon my honour,' said Mr Pickwick, nodding his head so energetically that the tassel of his night-cap danced again. 'I am almost ready to sink, Ma'am, beneath the confusion of addressing a lady in my night-cap (here the lady hastily snatched off hers), but I can't get it off, Ma'am (here Mr Pickwick gave it a tremendous tug, in proof of the statement). It is evident to me, Ma'am, now, that I have mistaken this bed-room for my own. I had not been here five minutes, Ma'am, when you suddenly entered it.'

'If this improbable story be really true, sir,' said the lady, sobbing violently, 'you will leave it instantly.'

'I will, Ma'am, with the greatest pleasure,' replied Mr Pickwick.

'Instantly, sir,' said the lady.

'Certainly, Ma'am,' interposed Mr Pickwick very quickly. 'Certainly, Ma'am. I – I – am very sorry, Ma'am,' said Mr Pickwick, making his appearance at the bottom of the bed, 'to have been the innocent occasion of this alarm and emotion; deeply sorry, Ma'am.'

The lady pointed to the door. One excellent quality of Mr Pickwick's character was beautifully displayed at this moment, under the most trying circumstances. Although he had hastily put on his hat over his night-cap, after the manner of the old patrol; although he carried his shoes and gaiters in his hand, and his coat and waistcoat over his arm; nothing could subdue his native politeness.

'I am exceedingly sorry, Ma'am,' said Mr Pickwick, bowing very low.

'If you are, sir, you will at once leave the room,' said the lady.

'Immediately, Ma'am; this instant, Ma'am,' said Mr Pickwick, opening the door, and dropping both his shoes with a crash in so doing.

'I trust, Ma'am,' resumed Mr Pickwick, gathering up his shoes, and turning round to bow again: 'I trust, Ma'am, that my unblemished character, and the devoted respect I entertain for your sex, will plead as some slight excuse for this' – But before Mr Pickwick could conclude the sentence the lady had thrust him into the passage, and locked and bolted the door behind him.

The Pickwick Papers, 1836–7

Strongly Illustrative of the Position, That the Course of True Love is Not a Railway: Dickens in Love

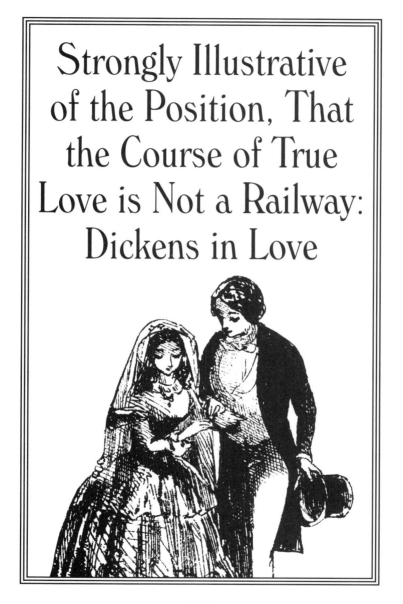

DICKENS FIRST FELL IN LOVE in 1829 when, at the age of seventeen, he met a young woman called Maria Beadnell. It was an unrequited affair; his affections were not reciprocated, in addition to which Maria's father, a banker, having discovered that Dickens's father had spent time in the Marshalsea, was against the match. Heartbroken, Dickens swore he would never fall in love again – but three years later he met and married Catherine Hogarth, with whom he had ten children. During their courtship he sent Catherine many sweet letters abounding with little endearments such as: 'dearest love', 'Dearest darling Pig', 'My dearest Wig' and 'Dearest Titmouse', but after they were married in 1836, rather than going to live by themselves, a third party joined them – Mary, Catherine's younger sister.

Mary was in awe of her brother-in-law and he of her. He constantly talked of her intelligence and beauty and at one point he describes her by saying she was not only 'the grace and life of our home' but also 'so perfect a creature' as 'never breathed'. Tragically however, in May 1837, after returning from the theatre, Mary was suddenly taken ill (the doctors later said it was a heart attack) and died in Dickens's arms. Afterwards Dickens insisted on keeping all of Mary's clothes so that he could look at them when the whim took him, and he also said that he longed to be buried beside her. In fact Mary's death was so devastating that Dickens never truly recovered. Mary came to represent an idealized picture of womanhood, one that Dickens used again and again in his novels when writing of virginal young girls, but most notably in the character of Little Nell in *The Old Curiosity Shop*.

And, what of his marriage? Dickens remained with Catherine for twenty-two years – although the two were never ideally suited, Catherine being a cautious, nervous woman, prone to fits of sullen behaviour as well as suffering from post-natal depression, while Dickens was very out-going, humorous, buoyant and quick-witted. In *David Copperfield*, his most autobiographical work, Dickens describes how the young David feels trapped by his wife . . . 'The old unhappy feeling,' he writes, 'pervaded my life. It was deepened, if it were changed at all; but it was as undefined as ever, and addressed me like a strain of sorrowful music faintly heard in the night. I loved my wife dearly, and I was happy; but the happiness I had vaguely anticipated, once, was not the happiness I enjoyed, and there was always something wanting.'

That there was 'something wanting' in his own marriage was underlined only too clearly when, at the age of forty-six, Dickens met and fell in love with an eighteen-year-old actress called Ellen Ternan. This was the final nail in the coffin of the Dickens's marriage and in 1858 he and Catherine separated. Their divorce was a bitter one with all sorts of allegations being made against Dickens, including one claim that he had committed incest with his sister-in-law, Georgina Hogarth (an allegation that was later proved unfounded). However, by that time the damage was done. 'My father,' wrote Dickens's daughter 'was like a madman . . . This affair brought out all that was worst – all that was weakest in him. He did not care a damn what happened to any of us.'

Finally Dickens secured his divorce and he and Ellen Ternan continued seeing each other until the late 1860s when Dickens's health took a turn for the worse.

To say that Dickens was a romantic when it came to writing about love is an understatement as several of his novels prove, but as the following quotations attest, Dickens also had a wicked sense of humour concerning matters of the heart.

'. . . *we* know, Mr Weller – we, who are men of the world – that a good uniform must work its way with the women, sooner or later.'

'The gentleman in blue',
The Pickwick Papers, 1846–7

❀

Refused! refused by a teacher, picked up by advertisement, at an annual salary of five pounds payable at indefinite periods, and 'found' in food and lodging like the very boys themselves . . .

Nicholas Nickleby, 1838–9

❀

'The state of my feelings towards Miss Dombey is of that unspeakable description, that my heart is a desert island, and she lives in it alone. I'm getting more used up every day, and I'm proud to be so. If you could see my legs when I take my boots off, you'd form some idea of what unrequited affection is.'

Mr Toots, *Dombey and Son*, 1846–8

❀

'She's a very charming and delightful creature,' quoth Mr Robert Sawyer, in reply; 'and has only one fault that I know of, Ben. It happens, unfortunately, that that single blemish is a want of taste. She don't like me.'

The Pickwick Papers, 1846–7

Love, however, is very materially assisted by a warm and active imagination: which has a long memory, and will thrive, for a considerable time, on very slight and sparing food.

Nicholas Nickleby, 1838–9

※

It was understood that nothing of a tender nature could possibly be confided to old Barley, by reason of his being totally unequal to the consideration of any subject more psychological than gout, rum, and purser's stores.

Great Expectations, 1860–1

※

Dombey and Son had often dealt in hides, but never in hearts. They left that fancy ware to boys and girls, and boarding-schools and books. Mr Dombey would have reasoned: That a matrimonial alliance with himself *must*, in the nature of things, be gratifying and honourable to any woman of common sense. That the hope of giving birth to a new partner in such a house, could not fail to awaken a glorious and stirring ambition in the breast of the least ambitious of her sex.

Dombey and Son, 1846–8

※

'There are strings,' said Mr Tappertit . . . 'in the human heart that had better not be wibrated.'

Simon Tappertit, *Barnaby Rudge*, 1841

'Cows are my passion. What I have ever sighed for, has been to retreat to a Swiss farm, and live entirely surrounded by cows – and china.'

Mrs Skewton, *Dombey and Son*, 1846–8

'And how, my sweet Miss Pecksniff,' said she [Mrs Todgers], 'how is your princely pa?'

Miss Pecksniff signified (in confidence) that he contemplated the introduction of a princely ma; and repeated the sentiment that she wasn't blind, and wasn't quite a fool, and wouldn't bear it.

Martin Chuzzlewit, 1843–4

I discovered afterwards that Miss Lavinia was an authority in affairs of the heart, by reason of there having anciently existed a certain Mr Pidger, who played short whist, and was supposed to have been enamoured of her. My private opinion is, that this was entirely a gratuitous assumption, and that Pidger was altogether innocent of any such sentiments – to which he had never given any sort of expression that I could ever hear of. Both Miss Lavinia and Miss Clarissa had a superstition, however, that he would have declared his passion, if he had not been cut short in his youth (at about sixty) by over-drinking his constitution, and over-doing an attempt to set it right again by swilling Bath water.

David, *David Copperfield*, 1849–50

'Oh, there's Ma being awful with somebody with a glass in his eye! Oh, I know she's going to bring him here! Oh, don't bring him, don't bring him! Oh, he'll be my partner with his glass in his eye! Oh, what shall I do?' This time Georgiana accompanied her ejaculations with taps of her feet upon the floor, and was altogether in quite a desperate condition. But, there was no escape from the majestic Mrs Podsnap's production of an ambling stranger, with one eye screwed up into extinction, and the other framed and glazed, who, having looked down out of that organ, as if he descried Miss Podsnap at the bottom of some perpendicular shaft, brought her to the surface, and ambled off with her.

Our Mutual Friend, 1864–5

※

'Mrs Norton is perhaps the most beautiful, but the Duchess, to my mind, is the more kissable.'

Observation of Charles Dickens in America, 1842

※

On the seventh night of cribbage, when Mrs Todgers, sitting by, proposed that instead of gambling they should play for 'love', Mr Moddle was seen to change colour. On the fourteenth night, he kissed Miss Pecksniff's snuffers, in the passage, when she went upstairs to bed: meaning to have kissed her hand, but missing it.

In short, Mr Moddle began to be impressed with the idea that Miss Pecksniff's mission was to comfort him; and Miss Pecksniff began to speculate on the probability of its being her mission to become ultimately Mrs Moddle.

Martin Chuzzlewit, 1843–4

Bumblings

George Cruikshank

A MONGST DICKENS'S HOST of lesser characters such as the Squeerses, the Pecksniffs, the Quilps, Heeps, Scrooges and Smallweeds, Mr Bumble, the workhouse beadle from *Oliver Twist* is one of his most successful creations.

Dickens loathed petty officials; he hated their hypocrisy, their bigotry, their misplaced dogmatism and, most of all, the way they wielded power over those less fortunate than themselves. He was also very well acquainted with the iniquities of a society in which workhouses weren't so much places of safety as breeding grounds for malnutrition and disease (in 1839 nearly half the deaths in London were of children under the age of ten). All of these things were integrated by Dickens one way or another into *Oliver Twist* – indeed the scenes set in the workhouse were nothing less than a scathing indictment of the new Poor Law of 1834 – but with the character of Bumble, Dickens surpassed himself, using as he did caricature and burlesque to strengthen his arguments and give his comedy a bite seldom attempted before.

But, tears were not the things to find their way to Mr Bumble's soul; his heart was waterproof. Like washable beaver hats that improve with rain, his nerves were rendered stouter and more vigorous, by showers of tears, which, being tokens of weakness, and so far tacit admissions of his own power, pleased and exalted him. He eyed his good lady with looks of great satisfaction, and begged, in an encouraging manner, that she should cry her hardest: the exercise being looked upon, by the faculty, as strongly conducive to health.

'It opens the lungs, washes the countenance, exercises the eyes, and softens down the temper,' said Mr Bumble. 'So cry away.'

As he discharged himself of this pleasantry, Mr Bumble took his hat from a peg, and putting it on, rather rakishly, on one side, as a man might, who felt he had asserted his superiority in a becoming manner, thrust his hands into his pockets, and sauntered towards the door, with much ease and waggishness depicted in his whole appearance.

Now, Mrs Corney that was, had tried the tears, because they were less troublesome than a manual assault; but, she was quite prepared to make trial of the latter mode of proceeding, as Mr Bumble was not long in discovering.

The first proof he experienced of the fact, was conveyed in a hollow sound, immediately succeeded by the sudden flying off of his hat to the opposite end of the room. This preliminary proceeding laying bare his head, the expert lady, clasping him tightly round the throat with one hand, inflicted a shower of blows (dealt with singular vigour and dexterity) upon it with the other. This done, she created a little variety by scratching his face, and tearing his hair; and, having, by this time, inflicted as much punishment as she deemed necessary for the offence, she pushed him over a chair, which was luckily well situated for the purpose: and defied him to talk about his prerogative again, if he dared.

'Get up!' said Mrs Bumble, in a voice of command. 'And take yourself away from here, unless you want me to do something desperate.'

Mr Bumble rose with a very rueful countenance: wondering much what something desperate might be. Picking up his hat, he looked towards the door.

'Are you going?' demanded Mrs Bumble.

'Certainly, my dear, certainly,' rejoined Mr Bumble, making a quicker motion towards the door. 'I didn't

intend to – I'm going, my dear! You are so very violent, that really I – '

At this instant, Mrs Bumble stepped hastily forward to replace the carpet, which had been kicked up in the scuffle. Mr Bumble immediately darted out of the room, without bestowing another thought on his unfinished sentence: leaving the late Mrs Corney in full possession of the field.

Mr Bumble was fairly taken by surprise, and fairly beaten. He had a decided propensity for bullying: derived no inconsiderable pleasure from the exercise of petty cruelty; and, consequently, was (it is needless to say) a coward. This is by no means a disparagement to his character; for many official personages, who are held in high respect and admiration, are the victims of similar infirmities. The remark is made, indeed, rather in his favour than otherwise, and with a view of impressing the reader with a just sense of his qualifications for office.

But, the measure of his degradation was not yet full. After making a tour of the house, and thinking, for the first time, that the poor-laws really were too hard on people; and that men who ran away from their wives, leaving them chargeable to the parish, ought, in justice, to be visited with no punishment at all, but rather rewarded as meritorious individuals who had suffered much; Mr Bumble came to a room where some of the female paupers were usually employed in washing the parish linen: whence the sound of voices in conversation, now proceeded.

'Hem!' said Mr Bumble, summoning up all his native dignity. 'These women at least shall continue to respect the prerogative. Hallo! hallo there! What do you mean by this noise, you hussies?'

With these words, Mr Bumble opened the door, and walked in with a very fierce and angry manner: which was at once exchanged for a most humiliated and cowering air, as his eyes unexpectedly rested on the form of his lady wife.

'My dear,' said Mr Bumble, 'I didn't know you were here.'

'Didn't know I was here!' repeated Mrs Bumble. 'What do YOU do here?'

'I thought they were talking rather too much to be doing their work properly, my dear,' replied Mr Bumble: glancing distractedly at a couple of old women at the wash-tub, who were comparing notes of admiration at the workhouse-master's humility.

'YOU thought they were talking too much?' said Mrs Bumble. 'What business is it of yours?'

George Cruikshank

'Why, my dear – ' urged Mr Bumble submissively.

'What business is it of yours?' demanded Mrs Bumble, again.

'It's very true, you're matron here, my dear,' submitted Mr Bumble; 'but I thought you mightn't be in the way just then.'

'I'll tell you what, Mr Bumble,' returned his lady. 'We don't want any of your interference. You're a great deal too fond of poking your nose into things that don't concern you, making everybody in the house laugh, the moment your back is turned, and making yourself look like a fool every hour in the day. Be off; come!'

Mr Bumble, seeing with excruciating feelings, the delight of the two old paupers, who were tittering together most rapturously, hesitated for an instant. Mrs Bumble, whose patience brooked no delay, caught up a bowl of soap-suds, and motioning him towards the door, ordered him instantly to depart, on pain of receiving the contents upon his portly person.

What could Mr Bumble do? He looked dejectedly round, and slunk away; and, as he reached the door, the titterings of the paupers broke into a shrill chuckle of irrepressible delight. It wanted but this. He was degraded in their eyes; he had lost caste and station before the very paupers; he had fallen from all the height and pomp of beadleship, to the lowest depth of the most snubbed henpeckery.

'All in two months!' said Mr Bumble, filled with dismal thoughts. 'Two months! No more than two months ago, I was not only my own master, but everybody else's, so far as the porochial workhouse was concerned, and now! –'

Oliver Twist, 1837–9

He Had But One Eye: Dickens's Characters

O^F all the outstanding features of a Dickens novel or short story, it is the vast array of characters that remain in the reader's mind long after finishing the book. In fact, with the exception of Shakespeare, I can think of no other author whose characters are part and parcel of the national consciousness as those of Charles Dickens. Think of Mr Micawber or Fagin, or Magwitch, not to mention Oliver Twist, David Copperfield or Scrooge. Characters and their small foibles were Dickens's meat and potatoes but, as he remarked on several occasions, none lived in his imagination until he had found them a name and so whenever he spied an interesting one (from a register perhaps, or from a gravestone) he would always take care to scribble it down in a notebook.

More than that, Dickens created characters by letting them evolve in his imagination. 'Suppose,' he once said to a group of friends, picking up a glass, 'Suppose I choose to call this a *character*, fancy it a man, endue it with certain qualities; and soon the fine filmy webs of thought, almost impalpable, coming from every direction, we know not whence, spin and weave about it, until it achieves form and beauty, and becomes instinct with life.' This process Dickens called the 'unfathomable mystery', but it must be due in part not only to the visual richness of his descriptions but also to his comic genius for summing people up as much through their faults as through anything else.

Mr Squeers's appearance was not prepossessing. He had but one eye, and the popular prejudice runs in favour of two.

Nicholas Nickleby, 1838–9

Mrs Joe was a very clean housekeeper, but had an exquisite art of making her cleanliness more uncomfortable and unacceptable than dirt itself.

Great Expectations, 1860–1

The man who now confronted Gashford, was a squat, thickset personage, with a low, retreating forehead, a coarse shock head of hair, and eyes so small and near together, that his broken nose alone seemed to prevent their meeting and fusing into one of the usual size.

Barnaby Rudge, 1841

. . . I had a latent impression that there was something decidedly fine in Mr Wopsle's elocution – not for old association's sake, I am afraid, but because it was very slow, very dreary, very up-hill and down-hill, and very unlike any way in which any man in any natural circumstances of life or death ever expressed himself about anything.

Pip, *Great Expectations*, 1860–1

Mr Barnacle dated from a better time, when the country was not so parsimonious, and the Circumlocution Office was not so badgered. He wound and wound folds of white cravat round his neck, as he wound and wound folds of tape and paper round the neck of the country.

Little Dorrit, 1855–7

Sooth to say, he was so wooden a man that he seemed to have taken his wooden leg naturally, and rather suggested to the fanciful observer that he might be expected – if his development received no untimely check – to be completely set up with a pair of wooden legs in about six months.

Our Mutual Friend, 1864–5, of Silas Wegg

Mr Chadband is a large yellow man, with a fat smile, and a general appearance of having a good deal of train oil in his system.

Bleak House, 1852–3

Mr Sparkler, stimulated by Love to brilliancy, replied that for a particular walk, a man ought to have a particular pair of shoes: as, for example, shooting, shooting-shoes; cricket, cricket-shoes. Whereas, he believed that Henry Gowan had no particular pair of shoes.

'No speciality?' said Mr Dorrit.

This being a very long word for Mr Sparkler, and his mind being exhausted by his late effort, he replied, 'No, thank you. I seldom take it.'

Little Dorrit, 1855–7

Most public characters have their failings; and the truth is that Mr Snevellicci was a little addicted to drinking; or, if the whole truth must be told, that he was scarcely ever sober. He knew in his cups three distinct stages of intoxication,– the dignified – the quarrelsome – the amorous. When professionally engaged he never got beyond the dignified; in private circles he went through all three, passing from one to another with a rapidity of transition often rather perplexing to those who had not the honour of his acquaintance.

Nicholas Nickleby, 1838–9

※

'That's a woman who observes and reflects in an uncommon manner. She's the sort of woman now,' said Mould, drawing his silk handkerchief over his head again, and composing himself for a nap 'one would almost feel disposed to bury for nothing: and do it neatly, too!'

Martin Chuzzlewit, 1843–4, of Sarah Gamp

※

Regarded as a classical ruin, Mrs Sparsit was an interesting spectacle on her arrival at her journey's end; but considered in any other light, the amount of damage she had by that time sustained was excessive, and impaired her claims to admiration.

Hard Times, 1854

※

'Any man may be in good spirits and good temper when he's well dressed. There ain't much credit in that.'

Mark Tapley, *Martin Chuzzlewit*, 1843–4

In his lifetime, and likewise in the period of Snagsby's 'time' of seven long years, there dwelt with Peffer, in the same law-stationering premises, a niece – a short, shrewd niece, something too violently compressed about the waist, and with a sharp nose like a sharp autumn evening, inclining to be frosty towards the end.

Bleak House, 1852–3

✤

'Annual income twenty pounds, annual expenditure nineteen nineteen six, result happiness. Annual income twenty pounds, annual expenditure twenty pounds ought and six, result misery. The blossom is blighted, the leaf is withered, the God of day goes down upon the dreary scene, and – and in short you are for ever floored. As I am!'

Mr Micawber, *David Copperfield*, 1849–50

✤

'Dumb as a drum vith a hole in it, sir.'

Sam Weller, *The Pickwick Papers*, 1836–7

✤

'Warm weather, Mrs Lammle,' said Fascination Fledgeby. Mrs Lammle thought it scarcely as warm as it had been yesterday. 'Perhaps not,' said Fascination Fledgeby with great quickness of repartee; 'but I expect it will be devilish warm to-morrow.'

Our Mutual Friend, 1864–5

'Blood cannot be obtained from a stone, neither can any-thing on account be obtained at present (not to mention law expenses) from Mr Micawber.'

Mrs Micawber, *David Copperfield*, 1849–50

❀

Mrs Varden was disposed to be amazingly cheerful. Indeed the worthy housewife was of such a capricious nature, that she not only attained a higher pitch of genius than Macbeth, in respect of her ability to be wise, amazed, temperate and furious, loyal and neutral in an instant, but would sometimes ring the changes backwards and for-wards on all possible moods and flights in one short quarter of an hour; performing, as it were, a kind of triple bob major on the peal of instruments in the female belfry, with a skilfulness and rapidity of execution that aston-ished all who heard her.

Barnaby Rudge, 1841

❀

'Ah! . . . he'd make a lovely corpse.'

Sarah Gamp, *Martin Chuzzlewit*, 1843–4, of a patient

❀

Why, Mr Bounderby was as near being Mr Gradgrind's bosom friend, as a man perfectly devoid of sentiment can approach that spiritual relationship towards another man perfectly devoid of sentiment. So near was Mr Bounderby – or, if the reader should prefer it, so far off.

He was a rich man: banker, merchant, manufacturer, and what not. A big, loud man, with a stare, and a metallic laugh. A man made out of a coarse material, which seemed to have been stretched to make so much of him. A man with a great puffed head and forehead, swelled veins in his temples, and such a strained skin to his face that it seemed to hold his eyes open, and lift his eyebrows up. A man with a pervading appearance on him of being inflated like a balloon, and ready to start. A man who could never sufficiently vaunt himself a self-made man. A man who was always proclaiming, through that brassy speaking trumpet of a voice of his, his old ignorance and his old poverty. A man who was the Bully of humility.

A year or two younger than his eminently practical friend, Mr Bounderby looked older; his seven or eight and forty might have had the seven or eight added to it again, without surprising anybody. He had not much hair. One might have fancied he had talked it off; and that what was left, all standing up in disorder, was in that condition from being constantly blown about by his windy boastfulness.

Hard Times, 1854

❈

First, there was Mr Spottletoe, who was so bald and had such big whiskers, that he seemed to have stopped his hair, by the sudden application of some powerful remedy, in the very act of falling off his head, and to have fastened it irrevocably on his face.

Martin Chuzzlewit, 1843–4

❈

Notwithstanding his very liberal laudation of himself, however, the Major was selfish. It may be doubted whether there ever was a more entirely selfish person at heart; or at stomach is perhaps a better expression, seeing that he was more decidedly endowed with that latter organ than with the former.

Dombey and Son, 1846–8

Of an ungainly make was Sloppy. Too much of him long-wise, too little of him broad-wise, and too many sharp angles of him angle-wise. One of those shambling male human creatures, born to be indiscreetly candid in the revelation of buttons . . .'

Our Mutual Friend, 1864–5

She was a fat old woman, this Mrs Gamp, with a husky voice and a moist eye, which she had a remarkable power of turning up, and only showing the white of it. Having very little neck, it cost her some trouble to look over her-self, if one may say so, at those to whom she talked. . . . The face of Mrs Gamp – the nose in particular – was some-what red and swollen, and it was difficult to enjoy her society without becoming conscious of a smell of spirits.

Martin Chuzzlewit, 1843–4

One might infer, from Judy's appearance, that her busi-ness rather lay with the thorns than the flowers . . .

Bleak House, 1852–3

'I needn't beg you,' [Mr Dombey] added, pausing for a moment at the settee before the fire, 'to take particular care of this young gentleman, Mrs . . .'

'Blockitt, Sir?' suggested the nurse, a simpering piece of faded gentility, who did not presume to state her name as a fact, but merely offered it as a mild suggestion.

Dombey and Son, 1846–8

Sim, as he was called in the locksmith's family, or Mr Simon Tappertit, as he called himself, and required all men to style him out of doors, on holidays, and Sundays out, – was an old-fashioned, thin-faced, sleek-haired, sharp-nosed, small-eyed little fellow, very little more than five feet high, and thoroughly convinced in his own mind that he was above the middle size; rather tall, in fact, than otherwise. Of his figure, which was well enough formed, though somewhat of the leanest, he entertained the highest admiration; and with his legs, which, in knee-breeches, were perfect curiosities of littleness, he was enraptured to a degree amounting to enthusiasm. He also had some majestic, shadowy ideas, which had never been quite fathomed by his intimate friends, concerning the power of his eye. Indeed he had been known to go so far as to boast that he could utterly quell and subdue the haughtiest beauty by a simple process, which he termed 'eyeing her over'; but it must be added, that neither of this faculty, nor of the power he claimed to have, through the same gift, of vanquishing and heaving down dumb animals, even in a rabid state, had he ever furnished evidence which could be deemed quite satisfactory and conclusive.

Barnaby Rudge, 1841

Sir Leicester Dedlock is only a baronet, but there is no
mightier baronet than he. His family is as old as the hills,
and infinitely more respectable. He has a general opinion
that the world might get on without hills, but would be
done up without Dedlocks.

Bleak House, 1852–3

❧

Now, Mr Bumble was a fat man, and a choleric; so,
instead of responding to this open-hearted salutation in a
kindred spirit, he gave the little wicket a tremendous
shake, and then bestowed upon it a kick which could have
emanated from no leg but a beadle's.

Oliver Twist, 1837–9

Of his architectural doings, nothing was clearly known, except that he had never designed or built anything; but it was generally understood that his knowledge of the science was almost awful in its profundity.

Martin Chuzzlewit, 1843–4, of Mr Pecksniff

❖

Mrs Micawber was quite as elastic. I have known her to be thrown into fainting fits by the King's taxes at three o'clock, and to eat lamb-chops, breaded, and drink warm ale (paid for with two teaspoons that had gone to the pawnbroker's) at four.

David, *David Copperfield*, 1849–50

❖

. . . although a skilful flatterer is a most delightful companion, if you can keep him all to yourself, his taste becomes very doubtful when he takes to complimenting other people.

Nicholas Nickleby, 1838–9

❖

Mr and Mrs Veneering were brand-new people in a brand-new house in a brand-new quarter in London. Everything about the Veneerings was spick-and-span new. All their furniture was new, all their friends were new, all their servants were new, their plate was new, their carriage was new, their harness was new, their horses were new, their pictures were new, they themselves were new, they were as newly married as was lawfully compatible with their having a brand-new baby, and, if they had set up a great-grandfather, he would have come home in matting from the Pantechnicon, without a scratch upon him, French polished to the crown of his head.

Our Mutual Friend, 1864–5

Mrs Varden was a lady of what is commonly called an uncertain temper – a phrase which being interpreted signifies a temper tolerably certain to make everybody more or less uncomfortable.

Barnaby Rudge, 1841

'Peggotty!' repeated Miss Betsey, with some indignation. 'Do you mean to say, child, that any human being has gone into a Christian church, and got herself named Peggotty?'

David Copperfield, 1849–50

'You are a pair of Whittingtons, gents, without the cat; which is a most agreeable and blessed exception to me, for I am not attached to the feline species. My name is Tigg; how do you do?'

Tigg Montague, *Martin Chuzzlewit*, 1843–4

It was not a bosom to repose upon, but it was a capital bosom to hang jewels upon.

Little Dorrit, 1855–7, of Mr Merdle

Demmit!

IN HIS LONG CAREER as both a novelist and playwright Charles Dickens created many wonderful characters, but none tickle the fancy in quite the same fashion as Mr Mantalini from *Nicholas Nickleby*.

Written shortly after *Oliver Twist*, *Nicholas Nickleby* as well as being a searing indictment of the 'Yorkshire schools' (institutions largely used for the dumping of illegitimate children), is also a comic masterpiece, containing such notable figures as the theatrical Mr and Mrs Crummles, alongside their daughter the 'Infant Phenomenon', Mrs Wititterly who spends much of her time reclining on a sofa and last, but certainly not least, Mrs Nickleby, who can never quite remember what she is talking about. Some people also regard the grotesque Squeers family as being comic and, in their way, they are (in particular poor Fanny Squeers). And, last but certainly not least, there is Mr Mantalini, whose improbable endearments towards his long-suffering wife, such as calling her his 'essential juice of pineapple', are second to none and read as freshly today as they must have done in Dickens's time.

'Let me see the names,' replied Ralph, impatiently extending his hand for the bills. 'Well! They are not sure, but they are safe enough. Do you consent to the terms, and will you take the money? I don't want you to do so. I would rather you didn't.'

'Demmit, Nickleby, can't you –' began Mr Mantalini.

'No,' replied Ralph, interrupting him. 'I can't. Will you take the money – down, mind; no delay, no going into the City and pretending to negotiate with some other party who has no existence, and never had. Is it a bargain, or is it not?'

Ralph pushed some papers from him as he spoke, and carelessly rattled his cash-box, as though by mere accident. The sound was too much for Mr Mantalini. He closed the bargain directly it reached his ears, and Ralph told the money out upon the table.

He had scarcely done so, and Mr Mantalini had not yet gathered it all up, when a ring was heard at the bell, and immediately afterwards Newman ushered in no less a person than Madame Mantalini, at sight of whom Mr Mantalini evinced considerable discomposure, and swept the cash into his pocket with remarkable alacrity.

'Oh, you *are* here,' said Madame Mantalini, tossing her head.

'Yes, my life and soul, I am,' replied her husband, dropping on his knees, and pouncing with kitten-like playfulness upon a stray sovereign. 'I am here, my soul's delight, upon Tom Tiddler's ground, picking up the demnition gold and silver.'

'I am ashamed of you,' said Madame Mantalini, with much indignation.

'Ashamed – of *me*, my joy? It knows it is talking demd charming sweetness, but naughty fibs,' returned Mr Mantalini. 'It knows it is not ashamed of its own popolorum tibby.'

Whatever were the circumstances which had led to such a result, it certainly appeared as though the popolorum tibby had rather miscalculated, for the nonce, the extent of his lady's affection. Madame Mantalini only looked scornful in reply; and, turning to Ralph, begged him to excuse her intrusion.

'Which is entirely attributable,' said Madame, 'to the gross misconduct and most improper behaviour of Mr Mantalini.'

'Of me, my essential juice of pineapple!'

'Of you,' returned his wife. 'But I will not allow it. I will not submit to be ruined by the extravagance and profligacy of any man. I call Mr Nickleby to witness the course I intend to pursue with you.'

'Pray don't call me to witness anything, ma'am,' said Ralph. 'Settle it between yourselves, settle it between yourselves.'

'No, but I must beg you as a favour,' said Madame Mantalini, 'to hear me give him notice of what it is my fixed intention to do – my fixed intention, sir,' repeated Madame Mantalini, darting an angry look at her husband.

'Will she call me "Sir"?' cried Mantalini. 'Me who dote upon her with the demdest ardour! She, who coils her fascinations round me like a pure angelic rattlesnake! It will be all up with my feelings; she will throw me into a demd state.'

'Don't talk of feelings, sir,' rejoined Madame Mantalini, seating herself, and turning her back upon him. 'You don't consider mine.'

'I do not consider yours, my soul!' exclaimed Mr Mantalini.

'No,' replied his wife.

And notwithstanding various blandishments on the part of Mr Mantalini, Madame Mantalini still said no, and said it too with such determined and resolute ill-temper, that Mr Mantalini was clearly taken aback.

'His extravagance, Mr Nickleby,' said Madame Mantalini, addressing herself to Ralph, who leant against his easy-chair with his hands behind him, and regarded the amiable couple with a smile of the supremest and most unmitigated contempt, – 'his extravagance is beyond all bounds.'

'I should scarcely have supposed it,' answered Ralph, sarcastically.

'I assure you, Mr Nickleby, however, that it is,' returned
Madame Mantalini. 'It makes me miserable! I am under
constant apprehensions, and in constant difficulty. And
even this,' said Madame Mantalini, wiping her eyes, 'is not
the worst. He took some papers of value out of my desk
this morning without asking my permission.'

Mr Mantalini groaned slightly, and buttoned his
trousers pocket.

'I am obliged,' continued Madame Mantalini, 'since
our late misfortunes, to pay Miss Knag a great deal of
money for having her name in the business, and I really

cannot afford to encourage him in all his wastefulness. As I have no doubt that he came straight here, Mr Nickleby, to convert the papers I have spoken of, into money, and as you have assisted us very often before, and are very much connected with us in this kind of matters, I wish you to know the determination at which his conduct has compelled me to arrive.'

Mr Mantalini groaned once more from behind his wife's bonnet, and fitting a sovereign into one of his eyes, winked with the other at Ralph. Having achieved this performance with great dexterity, he whipped the coin into his pocket, and groaned again with increased penitence.

'I have made up my mind,' said Madame Mantalini, as tokens of impatience manifested themselves in Ralph's countenance, 'to allowance him.'

'To do that, my joy?' inquired Mr Mantalini, who did not seem to have caught the words.

'To put him,' said Madame Mantalini, looking at Ralph, and prudently abstaining from the slightest glance at her husband, lest his many graces should induce her to falter in her resolution, 'to put him upon a fixed allowance; and I say that if he has a hundred and twenty pounds a year for his clothes and pocket-money, he may consider himself a very fortunate man.'

Mr Mantalini waited, with much decorum, to hear the amount of the proposed stipend, but when it reached his ears, he cast his hat and cane upon the floor, and drawing out his pocket-handkerchief, gave vent to his feelings in a dismal moan.

'Demnition!' cried Mr Mantalini, suddenly skipping out of his chair, and as suddenly skipping into it again, to the great discomposure of his lady's nerves. 'But no. It is a demd horrid dream. It is not reality. No!'

Comforting himself with this assurance, Mr Mantalini

closed his eyes and waited patiently till such time as he should wake up.

'A very judicious arrangement,' observed Ralph with a sneer, 'if your husband will keep within it, ma'am – as no doubt he will.'

'Demmit!' exclaimed Mr Mantalini, opening his eyes at the sound of Ralph's voice, 'it is a horrid reality. She is sitting there before me. There is the graceful outline of her form; it cannot be mistaken – there is nothing like it. The two countesses had no outlines at all, and the dowager's was a demd outline. Why is she so excruciatingly beautiful that I cannot be angry with her, even now?'

'You have brought it upon yourself, Alfred,' returned Madame Mantalini – still reproachfully, but in a softened tone.

'I am a demd villain!' cried Mr Mantalini, smiting himself on the head. 'I will fill my pockets with change for a sovereign in halfpence and drown myself in the Thames; but I will not be angry with her, even then, for I will put a note in the twopenny-post as I go along, to tell her where the body is. She will be a lovely widow. I shall be a body. Some handsome women will cry; she will laugh demnebly.'

'Alfred, you cruel, cruel creature,' said Madame Mantalini, sobbing at the dreadful picture.

'She calls me cruel – me – me – who for her sake will become a demd, damp, moist, unpleasant body!' exclaimed Mr Mantalini.

'You know it almost breaks my heart, even to hear you talk of such a thing,' replied Madame Mantalini.

'Can I live to be mistrusted?' cried her husband. 'Have I cut my heart into a demd extraordinary number of little pieces, and given them all away, one after another, to the same little engrossing demnition captivator, and can I live to be suspected by her? Demmit, no I can't.'

'Ask Mr Nickleby whether the sum I have mentioned is not a proper one,' reasoned Madame Mantalini.

'I don't want any sum,' replied her disconsolate husband; 'I shall require no demd allowance. I will be a body.'

On this repetition of Mr Mantalini's fatal threat, Madame Mantalini wrung her hands, and implored the interference of Ralph Nickleby; and after a great quantity of tears and talking, and several attempts on the part of Mr Mantalini to reach the door, preparatory to straightway committing violence upon himself, that gentleman was prevailed upon, with difficulty, to promise that he wouldn't be a body. This great point attained, Madame

Mantalini argued the question of the allowance, and Mr Mantalini did the same, taking occasion to show that he could live with uncommon satisfaction upon bread and water, and go clad in rags, but that he could not support existence with the additional burden of being mistrusted by the object of his most devoted and disinterested affection. This brought fresh tears into Madame Mantalini's eyes, which having just begun to open to some few of the demerits of Mr Mantalini, were only open a very little way, and could be easily closed again. The result was, that without quite giving up the allowance question, Madame Mantalini, postponed its further consideration; and Ralph saw, clearly enough, that Mr Mantalini had gained a fresh lease of his easy life, and that, for some time longer at all events, his degradation and downfall were postponed.

Nicholas Nickleby, 1838–9

I am Miserable: Husbands and Wives

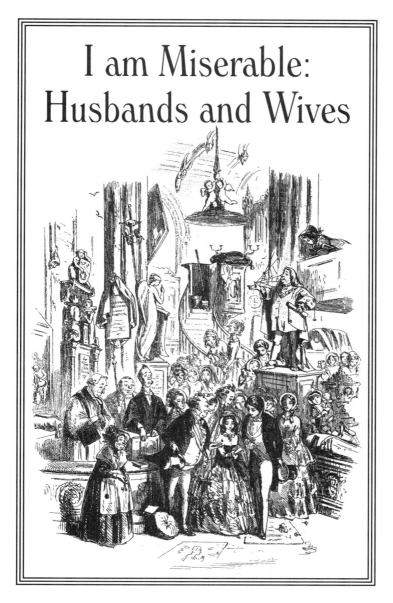

THAT DICKENS'S OWN MARRIAGE to Catherine Hogarth was not an entirely happy one is a well-documented fact. However, they *did* spend twenty-two years together and they *did* have ten children, so it is not unlikely that they enjoyed some happiness during this time. That being said, Catherine and Charles were not equally matched – indeed at one point Dickens wrote to his friend (and later his biographer) John Forster:

> Poor Catherine and I are not made for each other, and there is no help for it. It is not only that she makes me uneasy and unhappy, but that I make her so too – and much more so. She is exactly what you know, in the way of being amiable and complying; but we are strangely ill-assorted for the bond there is between us. God knows she would have been a thousand times happier if she had married another kind of man, and that her avoidance of this destiny would have been at least equally good for us both.

Other pressures on their partnership no doubt included the fact that over the course of their marriage Dickens turned from being an unknown writer into one of the most adored and famous men in the country, as well as the fact that two of Catherine's sisters (Mary and Georgina) came to live with them and, over a period of time, strongly endeared themselves to her husband.

Of his fictional partnerships, Mr and Mrs Lammle are perhaps the saddest and most sinister whereas Mr and Madame Mantalini emerge as the funniest. On the other hand Mr and Mrs Bumble run the Mantalinis a close second and Mr and Mrs Crummles, though not at each other's throats, make a splendidly humorous pair.

'I've found a sov'rin' cure for that, Sammy,' said Mr Weller, setting down the glass.

'A sovereign cure for the gout,' said Mr Pickwick hastily producing his note-book. 'What is it?'

'The gout, sir,' replied Mr Weller, 'the gout is a complaint as arises from too much ease and comfort. If ever you're attacked with the gout, sir, jist you marry a widder as has got a good loud voice, with a decent notion of usin' it, and you'll never have the gout agin.'

The Pickwick Papers, 1836–7

❀

'It runs in the family, I b'lieve, sir,' replied Mr Weller. 'My father's wery much in that line now. If my mother-in-law blows him up, he whistles. She flies in a passion and breaks his pipe; he steps out and gets another. Then she screams wery loud and falls into 'sterics; and he smokes wery comfortably till she comes to agin. That's philosophy, sir, ain't it?'

The Pickwick Papers, 1836–7

❀

'Are you going to sit snoring there, all day?' inquired Mrs Bumble.

'I am going to sit here, as long as I think proper, ma'am,' rejoined Mr Bumble; 'and although I was *not* snoring, I shall snore, gape, sneeze, laugh, or cry, as the humour strikes me; such being my prerogative.'

'*Your* prerogative!' sneered Mrs Bumble, with ineffable contempt.

'I said the word, ma'am,' said Mr Bumble. 'The prerogative of a man is to command.'

'And what's the prerogative of a woman, in the name of Goodness?' cried the relict of Mr Corney deceased.

'To obey, ma'am,' thundered Mr Bumble.

Oliver Twist, 1837–9

Beside him is a spare cushion, with which he is always provided, in order that he may have something to throw at the venerable partner of his respected age whenever she makes an allusion to money – a subject on which he is particularly sensitive.

'And where's Bart?' Grandfather Smallweed inquires of Judy, Bart's twin-sister.

'He ain't come in yet,' says Judy.

'It's his tea-time, isn't it?'

'No.'

'How much do you mean to say it wants then?'

'Ten minutes.'

'Hey?'

'Ten minutes.' (Loud on the part of Judy.)

'Ho!' says Grandfather Smallweed. 'Ten minutes.'

Grandmother Smallweed, who has been mumbling and shaking her head at the trivets, hearing figures mentioned, connects them with money, and screeches, like a horrible old parrot without any plumage, 'Ten, ten-pound notes!'

Grandfather Smallweed immediately throws the cushion at her.

'Drat you, be quiet!' says the good old man.

Bleak House, 1852–3

In this attitude he fell directly into a reverie, from which he was only aroused by his wife's calling to him from her ottoman, when they had been for some quarter-of-an-hour alone.

'Eh? Yes?' said Mr Merdle, turning towards her. 'What is it?'

'What is it?' repeated Mrs Merdle. 'It is, I suppose, that you have not heard a word of my complaint.'

'Your complaint, Mrs Merdle?' said Mr Merdle. 'I didn't know that you were suffering from a complaint. What complaint?'

'A complaint of you,' said Mrs Merdle.

'Oh! A complaint of me,' said Mr Merdle. 'What is the – what have I – what may you have to complain of in me, Mrs Merdle?'

In his withdrawing, abstracted, pondering way, it took him some time to shape this question. As a kind of faint attempt to convince himself that he was the master of the house, he concluded by presenting his forefinger to the parrot, who expressed his opinion on that subject by instantly driving his bill into it.

'You were saying, Mrs Merdle,' said Mr Merdle, with his wounded finger in his mouth, 'that you had a complaint against me?'

'A complaint which I could scarcely show the justice of more emphatically, than by having to repeat it,' said Mrs Merdle. 'I might as well have stated it to the wall. I had far better have stated it to the bird. He would at least have screamed.'

Little Dorrit, 1855–7

There was, however, the sound of voices in conversation in the next room; and as the conversation was loud and the partition thin, Kate could not help discovering that they belonged to Mr and Mrs Mantalini.

'If you will be odiously, demnebly, outrigeously jealous, my soul,' said Mr Mantalini, 'you will be very miserable – horrid miserable-demnition miserable.' And then, there came a sound as though Mr Mantalini were sipping his coffee.

'I *am* miserable,' returned Madame Mantalini, evidently pouting.

'Then you are an ungrateful, unworthy, demd unthankful little fairy,' said Mr Mantalini.

'I am not,' returned Madame, with a sob.

'Do not put itself out of humour,' said Mr Mantalini, breaking an egg. 'It is a pretty bewitching little demd countenance, and it should not be out of humour, for it spoils its loveliness, and makes it cross and gloomy like a frightful, naughty, demd hobgoblin.'

'I am not to be brought round in that way, always,' rejoined Madame, sulkily.

'It shall be brought round in any way it likes best, and not brought round at all if it likes that better,' retorted Mr Mantalini, with his egg-spoon in his mouth.

'It's very easy to talk,' said Mrs Mantalini.

'Not so easy when one is eating a demnition egg,' replied Mr Mantalini; 'for the yolk runs down the waist-coat, and yolk of egg does not match any waistcoat but a yellow waistcoat, demmit.'

'You were flirting with her during the whole night,' said Madame Mantalini, apparently desirous to lead the conversation back to the point from which it had strayed.

'No, no, my life.'

'You were,' said Madame; 'I had my eye upon you all the time.'

'Bless the little winking twinkling eye; was it on me all the time!' cried Mantalini, in a sort of lazy rapture. 'Oh, demmit!'

'And I say once more,' resumed Madame, 'that you ought not to waltz with anybody but your own wife; and I will not bear it, Mantalini, if I take poison first.'

'She will not take poison and have horrid pains, will she?' said Mantalini; who, by the altered sound of his voice, seemed to have moved his chair and taken up his position nearer to his wife. 'She will not take poison, because she had a demd fine husband who might have married two countesses and a dowager –'

'Two countesses,' interposed Madame. 'You told me one before!'

'Two!' cried Mantalini. 'Two demd fine women, real countesses and splendid fortunes, demmit.'

'And why didn't you?' asked Madame, playfully.

'Why didn't I!' replied her husband. 'Had I not seen, at a morning concert, the demdest little fascinator in all the world, and while that little fascinator is my wife, may not all the countesses and dowagers in England be –'

Mr Mantalini did not finish the sentence, but he gave Madame Mantalini a very loud kiss, which Madame Mantalini returned; after which, there seemed to be some more kissing mixed up with the progress of the breakfast.

Nicholas Nickleby, 1838–9

'. . . Look at her – mother of six children – three of 'em alive, and all upon the stage!'

'Extraordinary!' cried Nicholas.

'Ah! extraordinary indeed,' rejoined Mr Crummles, taking a complacent pinch of snuff, and shaking his head gravely. 'I pledge you my professional word I didn't even know she could dance, till her last benefit, and then she played Juliet, and Helen Macgregor, and did the skipping-rope hornpipe between the pieces. The very first time I saw that admirable woman, Johnson,' said Mr Crummles, drawing a little nearer, and speaking in the tone of confidential friendship, 'she stood upon her head on the butt-end of a spear, surrounded with blazing fireworks.'

'You astonish me!' said Nicholas.

'*She* astonished *me*!' returned Mr Crummles, with a very serious countenance. 'Such grace, coupled with such dignity! I adored her from that moment.'

Nicholas Nickleby, 1838–9

Mr and Mrs Lammle have walked for some time on the Shanklin sands, and one may see by their footprints that they have not walked arm in arm, and that they have not walked in a straight track, and that they have walked in a moody humour; for, the lady has prodded little spurting holes in the damp sand before her with her parasol, and the gentleman has trailed his stick after him. As if he were of the Mephistopheles family indeed, and had walked with a drooping tail.

Our Mutual Friend, 1864–5

Deformation of Character: Prison, Politics and the Law

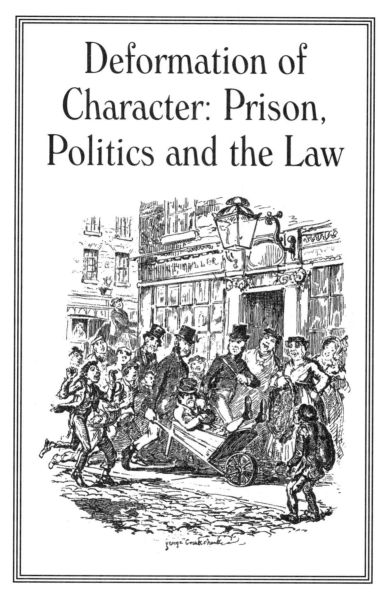

george Cruikshank

HAVING HAD first-hand experience of the Marshalsea Prison when his father was sent there for non-payment of debts and, having worked as a lawyer's clerk at Ellis & Blackmore for some time during his late teens, Dickens had a solid grounding when it came to describing both institutions. That he didn't hold either in high esteem (being a long-term campaigner for prison reform as well as a general champion of justice and human decency) ensured that in his novels both the law and the prison system came in for a great deal of criticism as well as a fair amount of lampooning.

Thus, in the midst of the mud, and at the heart of the fog, sits the Lord High Chancellor in his High Court of Chancery.

'Mr Tangle,' says the Lord High Chancellor, latterly something restless under the eloquence of that learned gentleman.

'Mlud,' says Mr Tangle. Mr Tangle knows more of Jarndyce and Jarndyce than anybody. He is famous for it – supposed never to have read anything else since he left school.

'Have you nearly concluded your argument?'

'Mlud, no – variety of points – feel it my duty tsubmit – ludship,' is the reply that slides out of Mr Tangle.

'Several members of the bar are still to be heard, I believe?' says the Chancellor, with a slight smile.

Eighteen of Mr Tangle's learned friends, each armed with a little summary of eighteen hundred sheets, bob up like eighteen hammers in a pianoforte, make eighteen bows, and drop into their eighteen places of obscurity.

'We will proceed with the hearing on Wednesday fort-night,' says the Chancellor. For the question at issue is only a question of costs, a mere bud on the forest tree of the parent suit, and really will come to a settlement one of these days.

Bleak House, 1852–3

The Circumlocution Office was (as everybody knows with-out being told) the most important Department under Government. No public business of any kind could possi-bly be done at any time, without the acquiescence of the Circumlocution Office. Its finger was in the largest public pie, and in the smallest public tart. It was equally impossi-ble to do the plainest right and to undo the plainest wrong, without the express authority of the Circumlocution Office. If another Gunpowder Plot had been discovered half an hour before the lighting of the match, nobody would have been justified in saving the parliament until there had been half a score of boards, half a bushel of minutes, several sacks of official memoranda, and a family-vault full of ungrammatical correspondence, on the part of the Circumlocution Office . . . Whatever was required to be done, the Circumlocution Office was beforehand with all the public departments in the art of perceiving – HOW NOT TO DO IT.

Little Dorrit, 1855–7

'Our member has come down express,' returned the land-lord. 'No scrubs would do for no such a purpose. Nothing less would satisfy our Directors than our member in the

House of Commons, who is returned upon the Gentlemanly Interest.'

'Which interest is that?' asked Martin.

'What, don't you know!' returned the landlord.

It was quite clear the landlord didn't. They always told
him at election time, that it was the Gentlemanly side, and
he immediately put on his top-boots, and voted for it.

Martin Chuzzlewit, 1843–4

'Silence there!' cried the jailer.

'What is this?' inquired one of the magistrates.

'A pick-pocketing case, your worship.'

'Has the boy ever been here before?'

'He ought to have been, a many times,' replied the
jailer. 'He has been pretty well everywhere else. *I* know
him well, your worship.'

'Oh! you know me, do you?' cried the Artful, making a
note of the statement. 'Wery good. That's a case of defor-
mation of character, any way.'

Oliver Twist, 1837–9

The mature young gentleman is a gentleman of property.
He invests his property. He goes in a condescending, ama-
teurish way into the City, attends meetings of the
Directors, and has to do with traffic in Shares. As is well
known to the wise in their generation, traffic in Shares is
the one thing to have to do with in this world. Have no
antecedents, no established character, no cultivation,
no ideas, no manners; have Shares. Have Shares enough
to be on Boards of Direction in capital letters, oscillate on

mysterious business between London and Paris, and be great. Where does he come from? Shares. Where is he going to? Shares. What squeezes him into Parliament? Shares. Perhaps he never of himself achieved success in anything, never originated anything, never produced anything? Sufficient answer to all: Shares. Oh, mighty Shares!

Our Mutual Friend, 1864–5

'It is an old prerogative of kings to govern everything but their passions.'

Mr Pickwick, reading from 'The True Legend of
Prince Bladud', *The Pickwick Papers*, 1836–7

'Slumkey forever!' roared the honest and the independent.

'Slumkey forever!' echoed Mr Pickwick, taking off his hat.

'No Fizkin!' roared the crowd.

'Certainly not!' shouted Mr Pickwick.

'Hurrah!' And then there was another roaring, like that of a whole menagerie when the elephant has rung the bell for the cold meat.

'Who is Slumkey?' whispered Mr Tupman.

'I don't know,' replied Mr Pickwick in the same tone. 'Hush. Don't ask any questions. It's always best on these occasions to do what the mob do.'

'But suppose there are two mobs?' suggested Mr Snodgrass.

'Shout with the largest,' replied Mr Pickwick.

Volumes could not have said more.

The Pickwick Papers, 1836–7

Oh heaven, if you could have been with me at a hospital dinner last Monday! There were men there – your City aristocracy – who made such speeches and expressed such sentiments as any moderately intelligent dustman would have blushed through his cindery bloom to have thought of. Sleek, slobbering, bow-paunched, over-fed, apoplectic, snorting cattle, and the auditory leaping up in their delight! I never saw such an illustration of the power of the purse, or felt so degraded and debased by its contemplation.

Letter from Charles Dickens
to Douglas Jerrold, 1842

※

'But you have not imparted to me,' remarks Veneering, 'what you think of my entering the House of Commons?' 'I think,' rejoins Twemlow, feelingly, 'that it is the best club in London.'

Our Mutual Friend, 1864–5

※

'It was as true . . . as turnips is. It was as true . . . as taxes is. And nothing's truer than them.'

Mr Barkis, *David Copperfield*, 1849–50

※

'If there's any illness when that wessel gets to sea,' said Mrs Gamp, prophetically, 'it's murder, and I'm a witness for the persecution.'

Martin Chuzzlewit, 1843–4

Always a campaigner for the underdog – in particular for children who were forced to work down the mines and in other equally horrendous places, Dickens wrote a series of lampoons on the Tories, the most cutting of which was a new version of 'The Fine Old English Gentleman'.

I'll sing you a new ballad, and I'll warrant it first-rate,
Of the days of that old gentleman who had that old
    estate;
When they spent the public money at a bountiful old rate
On ev'ry mistress, pimp, and scamp, at ev'ry noble gate,
In the fine old English Tory times;
Soon may they come again!

The good old laws were garnished well with gibbets,
    whips, and chains,
With fine old English penalties, and fine old English
    pains,
With rebel heads, and seas of blood once hot in rebel
    veins;
For all these things were requisite to guard the rich old
    gains
Of the fine old English Tory times;
Soon may they come again!

The bright old day now dawns again; the cry runs
    through the land,
In England there shall be – dear bread! in Ireland –
    sword and brand!
And poverty, and ignorance, shall swell the rich and
    grand,
So, rally round the rulers with the gentle iron hand,
Of the fine old English Tory days;
Hail to the coming time!

[96]

Americans Can't Bear to be Told Their Faults

IN JANUARY 1842 Charles Dickens, together with his wife, left England for a tour of America. It was a highly successful trip. Dickens was fêted by all and sundry – he met, amongst others, Henry Wadsworth Longfellow and Washington Irving; he attended banquets and balls, gave speeches and had an audience with the then President, John Tyler. 'I can give you no conception of my welcome here,' he wrote to his friend and confidant Thomas Mitton. 'There never was a king or emperor upon the earth so cheered and followed by crowds, and entertained in public at splendid balls and dinners . . .'

But Dickens did not just confine himself to pleasurable pursuits: he also visited mental asylums, prisons, workhouses, orphanages and even an institute for the blind, and he was not disappointed, finding as he did a more modern approach to social welfare than in his own United Kingdom. However, all was not sunshine and light in the New World; indeed there were more than a few hiccups along the way; one arising from Dickens's opinion that British authors were being cheated out of huge sums of money due to the American copyright laws. This led to an immediate outcry by the American press. 'It happens that we want no advice,' the *Hartford Times* wrote, 'on the subject and it will be better for Mr Dickens if he refrains from introducing the subject hereafter.'

This war of words continued throughout Dickens's visit and coloured his whole journey through America to the extent that Mary Shelley wrote a letter to a friend saying that 'Charles Dickens has just come home in a state of violent dislike of the Americans – and means to devour them in his next work – he says they are so frightfully dishonest.' His 'next work' was *American Notes*, quickly followed by *Martin Chuzzlewit* – both of which were quite scathing of America.

That being said, Dickens's trip was for the most part an experience that he relished and as he was to comment to John Forster, 'Oh! the sublimated essence of comicality that I *could* distil, from the materials I have!' The following excerpts are a few of Dickens's more humorous observations . . .

I believe that there is no country, on the face of the earth, where there is less freedom of opinion on any subject in reference to which there is a broad difference of opinion than in this. . . . There! I write the words with reluctance, disappointment, and sorrow; but I believe it from the bottom of my soul. . . . I tremble for a radical coming here, unless he is a radical on principle, by reason and reflection, and from the sense of right. I fear that if he were anything else, he would return home a tory . . . I do fear that the heaviest blow ever dealt at liberty will be dealt by this country, in the failure of its example.

Letter from Charles Dickens to John Forster, 1842

❖

'Is smartness American for forgery?' asked Martin.

'Well! said the colonel, 'I expect it's American for a good many things that you call by other names. But you can't help yourself in Europe. We can.'

'And do, sometimes,' thought Martin.

Martin Chuzzlewit, 1843–4

In the courts of law, the judge has his spittoon on the bench, the counsel have theirs, the witness has his, the prisoner his, and the crier his. The jury are accommodated at the rate of three men to a spittoon . . . I have twice seen gentlemen at evening parties in New York, turn aside when they were not engaged in conversation, and spit upon the drawing-room carpet. And in every barroom and hotel passage the stone floor looks as if it were paved with open oysters – from the quantity of this kind of deposit which tessellates it all over.

Observation of Charles Dickens in America, 1842

I see a press more mean, and paltry, and silly, and disgraceful than any country I ever knew. . . . I speak of Bancroft, and am advised to be silent on that subject, for he is 'a black sheep – a democrat'. I speak of Bryant, and am entreated to be more careful – for the same reason. I speak of international copyright, and am implored not to ruin myself outright. I speak of Miss Martineau, and all parties – Slave Upholders and Abolitionists, Whigs, Tyler Whigs, and Democrats, shower down upon her a perfect cataract of abuse.

'But what has she done? Surely she praised America enough!'

'Yes, but she told us some of our faults, and Americans can't bear to be told their faults.'

Letter from Charles Dickens
to William Charles Macready, 1842

You can never conceive what the hawking and spitting is, the whole night through. *Upon my honour and word* I was obliged, this morning, to lay my fur-coat on the deck, and wipe the half-dried flakes of spittle from it with my handkerchief: and the only surprise seemed to be, that I should consider it necessary to do so.

Letter from Charles Dickens to John Forster, 1842

There are not so many intensified bores as in these United States.

Observation of Charles Dickens, 1842

I really think my face has acquired a fixed expression of sadness from the constant and unmitigated boring I endure. . . . There is a line in my chin (on the right side of the underlip) indelibly fixed there by the New Englander . . . A dimple has vanished from my cheek, which I felt myself robbed of at the time by a wise legislator.

Dickens on his visit to America, 1842

Now the coach flung us in a heap on its floor, and now crushed our heads against its roof. . . . Still, the day was beautiful, the air delicious, and we were *alone*, with no tobacco spittle, or eternal prosy conversation about dollars and politics (the only two subjects they ever converse about, or can converse about) to bore us.

Observation of Charles Dickens, 1842

I don't think Anne (Kate's maid) has so much as seen an American tree. She objects to Niagara that, 'it's nothing but water and that there is too much of that.'

An observation of Charles Dickens
on his wife's maid, Anne, 1842

✦

English kindness is very different from American. People send their horses and carriages for your use, but they don't exact as payment the right of being always under your nose.

Observation of Charles Dickens, 1842

✦

Their [the American people's] demeanour is invariably morose, sullen, clownish and repulsive. I should think there is not, on the face of the earth, a people so entirely destitute of humour, vivacity, or the capacity of enjoyment.

Observation of Charles Dickens, 1842

✦

[Bill] 'All men are alike in the U-nited States, an't they? It makes no odds whether a man has a thousand pound, or nothing, there. Particular in New York, I'm told, where Ned landed.'

'New York, was it?' asked Martin, thoughtfully.

'Yes,' said Bill. 'New York. I know that, because he sent word home that it brought Old York to his mind, quite wivid, in consequence of being so exactly unlike it in every respect.'

Martin Chuzzlewit, 1843–4

Politics are much discussed, so are banks, so is cotton. Quiet people avoid the question of the Presidency . . . the great constitutional feature of this institution being, that directly the acrimony of the last election is over, the next one begins.

American Notes, 1842

❋

In all modes of travelling, the American customs, with reference to the means of personal cleanliness and wholesome ablution, are extremely negligent and filthy; and I strongly incline to the belief that a considerable amount of illness is referable to this cause.

American Notes, 1842

❋

. . . dyspeptic ladies and gentlemen . . . eat unheard-of quantities of hot corn bread (almost as good for the digestion as a kneaded pin-cushion), for breakfast, and for supper. Those who do not observe this custom, and who help themselves several times instead, usually suck their knives and forks meditatively, until they have decided what to take next: then pull them out of their mouths: put them in the dish; help themselves; and fall to work again. At dinner, there is nothing to drink upon the table, but great jugs full of cold water. Nobody says anything, at any meal, to anybody. All the passengers are very dismal, and seem to have tremendous secrets weighing on their minds. There is no conversation, no laughter, no cheerfulness, no sociality, except in spitting; and that is done in silent fellowship round the stove, when the meal is over.

American Notes, 1842

Aggrawation and Cowcumbers: The Inimitable Mrs Gamp

*M*artin *Chuzzlewit* was Dickens's sixth novel, appearing as it did in monthly instalments between the years 1843–4. Set in part in the United States, it mercilessly satirized that country, causing not a little consternation among Dickens's American readers (for instance Dickens gave the New York newspapers such ignominious names as the *Sewer*, the *Peeper* and the *Stabber*). That being said, the novel, although not such a resounding success as *The Pickwick Papers* or *Oliver Twist*, did eventually achieve some acclaim and in Britain at least became a favourite amongst Dickens's numerous readers. This must be due in part to two of the main characters – the hypocritical architect, Mr Pecksniff and the unforgettably grotesque midwife and nurse, Mrs Gamp, who attends 'a lying-in or a laying-out with equal zest and relish'. One of Dickens's 'larger than life' creations, she stands not just for the Victorian poor, but as a figure of almost mythical importance in an age when birth was precarious and death all too frequent.

The following scene takes place at Mrs Gamp's own place of residence, where she is expecting her fellow nurse, Betsey Prig for tea. When Mrs Prig turns up, Mrs Gamp has just been informed by her landlord of a murder . . .

———————◦◦◦◦◦◦———————

At this juncture the little bell rang, and the deep voice of Mrs Prig struck into the conversation.

'Oh! You're a-talkin' about it, are you!' observed that lady. 'Well, I hope you've got it over, for I ain't interested in it myself.'

'My precious Betsey,' said Mrs Gamp, 'how late you are!'

The worthy Mrs Prig replied, with some asperity, 'that

if perwerse people went off dead, when they was least expected, it warn't no fault of her'n.' And further, 'that it was quite aggrawation enough to be made late when one was dropping for one's tea, without hearing on it again.'

Mrs Gamp, deriving from this exhibition of repartee some clue to the state of Mrs Prig's feelings, instantly conducted her upstairs; deeming that the sight of pickled salmon might work a softening change.

But Betsey Prig expected pickled salmon. It was obvious that she did; for her first words, after glancing at the table, were:

'I know'd she wouldn't have a cowcumber!'

Mrs Gamp changed colour, and sat down upon the bedstead.

'Lord bless you, Betsey Prig, your words is true. I quite forgot it!'

Mrs Prig, looking steadfastly at her friend, put her hand in her pocket, and with an air of surly triumph drew forth either the oldest of lettuces or youngest of cabbages, but at any rate, a green vegetable of an expansive nature, and of such magnificent proportions that she was obliged to shut it up like an umbrella before she could pull it out. She also produced a handful of mustard and cress, a trifle of the herb called dandelion, three bunches of radishes, an onion rather larger than an average turnip, three substantial slices of beetroot, and a short prong or antler of celery; the whole of this garden-stuff having been publicly exhibited, but a short time before, as a twopenny salad, and purchased by Mrs Prig on condition that the vendor could get it all into her pocket. Which had been happily accomplished, in High Holborn, to the breathless interest of a hackney-coach stand. And she laid so little stress on this surprising forethought, that she did not even smile, but returning her pocket into its accustomed sphere, merely recommended that these productions of nature should be sliced up, for immediate consumption, in plenty of vinegar.

'And don't go a-droppin' none of your snuff in it,' said Mrs Prig. 'In gruel, barley-water, apple-tea, mutton-broth, and that, it don't signify. It stimulates a patient. But I don't relish it myself.'

'Why, Betsey Prig!' cried Mrs Gamp, 'how *can* you talk so!'

'Why, ain't your patients, wotever their diseases is, always asneezin' their wery heads off, along of your snuff?' said Mrs Prig.

'And wot if they are!' said Mrs Gamp

'Nothing if they are,' said Mrs Prig. 'But don't deny it, Sairah.'

'Who deniges of it?' Mrs Gamp inquired.

Mrs Prig returned no answer.

'*Who* deniges of it, Betsey?' Mrs Gamp inquired again. Then Mrs Gamp, by reversing the question, imparted a deeper and more awful character of solemnity to the same. 'Betsey, who deniges of it?'

It was the nearest possible approach to a very decided difference of opinion between these ladies; but Mrs Prig's impatience for the meal being greater at the moment than her impatience of contradiction, she replied, for the present, 'Nobody, if you don't, Sairah,' and prepared herself for tea. For a quarrel can be taken up at any time, but a limited quantity of salmon cannot.

Her toilet was simple. She had merely to 'chuck' her bonnet and shawl upon the bed; give her hair two pulls, one upon the right side and one upon the left, as if she were ringing a couple of bells; and all was done. The tea was already made, Mrs Gamp was not long over the salad, and they were soon at the height of their repast.

The temper of both parties was improved, for the time being, by the enjoyments of the table. When the meal came to a termination (which it was pretty long in doing), and Mrs Gamp having cleared away, produced the teapot from the top shelf, simultaneously with a couple of wineglasses, they were quite amiable.

'Betsey,' said Mrs Gamp, filling her own glass and passing the teapot, 'I will now propoge a toast. My frequent pardner, Betsey Prig!'

'Which, altering the name to Sairah Gamp; I drink,' said Mrs Prig, 'with love and tenderness.'

From this moment symptoms of inflammation began to lurk in the nose of each lady; and perhaps, notwithstanding all appearances to the contrary, in the temper also.

'Now, Sairah,' said Mrs Prig, 'joining business with pleasure, wot is this case in which you wants me?'

Mrs Gamp betraying in her face some intention of returning an evasive answer, Betsey added:

'*Is* it Mrs Harris?'

'No, Betsey Prig, it ain't,' was Mrs Gamp's reply.

'Well!' said Mrs Prig, with a short laugh. 'I'm glad of that, at any rate.'

'Why should you be glad of that, Betsey?' Mrs Gamp retorted, warmly. 'She is unbeknown to you except by hearsay, why should you be glad? If you have anythink to say contrairy to the character of Mrs Harris, which well I knows behind her back, afore her face, or anywheres, is not to be impeaged, out with it, Betsey. I have know'd that sweetest and best of women,' said Mrs Gamp, shaking her head, and shedding tears, 'ever since afore her First, which Mr Harris who was dreadful timid went and stopped his ears in a empty dog-kennel, and never took his hands away or come out once till he was showed the baby, wen bein' took with fits, the doctor collared him and laid him on his back upon the airy stones, and she was told to ease her mind, his owls was organs. And I have know'd her, Betsey Prig, when he has hurt her feelin' art by sayin' of his Ninth that it was one too many, if not two, while that dear innocent was cooin' in his face, which thrive it did though bandy, but I have never know'd as you had occagion to be glad, Betsey, on accounts of Mrs Harris not requiring you. Require she never will, depend upon it, for her constant words in sickness is, and will be, "Send for Sairey?"'

During this touching address, Mrs Prig adroitly feigning to be the victim of that absence of mind which has its origin in excessive attention to one topic, helped herself from the teapot without appearing to observe it. Mrs Gamp observed it, however, and came to a premature close in consequence.

'Well, it ain't her, it seems,' said Mrs Prig, coldly; 'who is it then?'

'You have heerd me mention, Betsey,' Mrs Gamp replied, after glancing in an expressive and marked manner at the tea-pot, 'a person as I took care on at the time as you and me was pardners off and on, in that there fever at the Bull?'

'Old Snuffey,' Mrs Prig observed.

Sarah Gamp looked at her with an eye of fire, for she saw in this mistake of Mrs Prig, another wilful and malignant stab at that same weakness or custom of hers, an ungenerous allusion to which, on the part of Betsey, had first disturbed their harmony that evening. And she saw it still more clearly, when, politely but firmly correcting that lady by the distinct enunciation of the word 'Chuffey', Mrs Prig received the correction with a diabolical laugh.

The best among us have their failings, and it must be conceded of Mrs Prig, that if there were a blemish in the goodness of her disposition, it was a habit she had of not bestowing all its sharp and acid properties upon her patients (as a thoroughly amiable woman would have done), but of keeping a considerable remainder for the service of her friends. Highly pickled salmon, and lettuces chopped up in vinegar, may, as viands possessing some acidity of their own, have encouraged and increased this failing in Mrs Prig; and every application to the teapot certainly did; for it was often remarked of her by her friends, that she was most contradictory when most elevated. It is certain that her countenance became about this time derisive and defiant, and that she sat with her arms folded, and one eye shut up, in a somewhat offensive, because obstrusively intelligent, manner.

Mrs Gamp observing this, felt it the more necessary that Mrs Prig should know her place, and be made sensible of her exact station in society, as well as of her obligations to herself. She therefore assumed an air of greater patronage and importance, as she went on to answer Mrs Prig a little more in detail.

'Mr Chuffey, Betsey,' said Mrs Gamp, 'is weak in his mind. Excuge me if I makes remark, that he may neither be so weak as people thinks, nor people may not think he is so weak as they pretends, and what I knows, I knows; and what you don't, you don't; so do not ask me, Betsey. But Mr Chuffey's friends has made propojals for his bein' took care on, and has said to me, "Mrs Gamp, *will* you undertake it? We couldn't think," they says, "of trusting him to nobody but you, for, Sairey, you are gold as has passed the furnage. Will you undertake it, at your own price, day and night, and by your own self?" "No," I says, "I will not. Do not reckon on it. There is," I says, "but one creetur in the world as I would undertake on sech terms, and her name is Harris. But" I says, "I am acquainted with a friend, whose name is Betsey Prig, that I can recommend, and will assist me. Betsey," I says, "is always to be trusted, under me, and will be guided as I could desire."'

Here Mrs Prig, without any abatement of her offensive manner again counterfeited abstraction of mind, and stretched out her hand to the tea-pot. It was more than Mrs Gamp could bear. She stopped the hand of Mrs Prig with her own, and said, with great feeling:

'No, Betsey! Drink fair, wotever you do!'

Mrs Prig, thus baffled, threw herself back in her chair, and closing the same eye more emphatically, and folding her arms tighter, suffered her head to roll slowly from side to side, while she surveyed her friend with a contemptuous smile.

Mrs Gamp resumed:

'Mrs Harris, Betsey –'

'Bother Mrs Harris!' said Betsey Prig.

Mrs Gamp looked at her with amazement, incredulity, and indignation; when Mrs Prig, shutting her eye still closer, and folding her arms still tighter, uttered these memorable and tremendous words:

'I don't believe there's no sich a person!'

After the utterance of which expressions, she leaned forward, and snapped her fingers once, twice, thrice; each time nearer to the face of Mrs Gamp, and then rose to put on her bonnet, as one who felt that there was now a gulf between them, which nothing could ever bridge across.

The shock of this blow was so violent and sudden, that Mrs Gamp sat staring at nothing with uplifted eyes, and her mouth open as if she were gasping for breath, until Betsey Prig had put on her bonnet and her shawl, and was gathering the latter about her throat. Then Mrs Gamp rose – morally and physically rose – and denounced her.

'What!' said Mrs Gamp, 'you bage creetur, have I know'd Mrs Harris five and thirty year, to be told at last that there ain't no sech a person livin'! Have I stood her friend in all her troubles, great and small, for it to come at last to sech a end as this, which her own sweet picter hanging up afore you all the time, to shame your Bragian words! But well you mayn't believe there's no sech a creetur, for she wouldn't demean herself to look at you, and often has she said, when I have made mention of your name, which, to my sinful sorrow, I have done, "What, Sairey Gamp! debage yourself to *her*!" Go along with you!'

Martin Chuzzlewit, 1843–4

Flopping

A Tale of Two Cities (1859) is without doubt Dickens's greatest historical work. Written during a time of great upheaval in his own life – he had just left his wife and children – it is one of his most sombre books.

The novel is set in both London and Paris and, although ostensibly a love story, it is also a chilling account of the Terror, during which time so many French citizens were imprisoned and guillotined. With that as the backdrop one might suspect that there is little humour to be found in the book. However, as with any of Dickens's greatest work, comedy is not far from the surface and the following scene is one of Dickens's finest.

Mr Cruncher's apartments were not in a savoury neighbourhood, and were but two in number, even if a closet with a single pane of glass in it might be counted as one. But they were very decently kept. Early as it was, on the windy March morning, the room in which he lay abed was already scrubbed throughout; and between the cups and saucers arranged for breakfast, and the lumbering deal table, a very clean white cloth was spread.

Mr Cruncher reposed under a patchwork counterpane, like a Harlequin at home. At first, he slept heavily, but, by degrees, began to roll and surge in bed, until he rose above the surface, with his spiky hair looking as if it must tear the sheets to ribbons. At which juncture, he exclaimed, in a voice of dire exasperation:

'Bust me, if she ain't at it agin!'

A woman of orderly and industrious appearance rose from her knees in a corner, with sufficient haste and trepidation to show that she was the person referred to.

'What!' said Mr Cruncher, looking out of bed for a boot. 'You're at it agin, are you?'

After hailing the morn with this second salutation, he threw a boot at the woman as a third. It was a very muddy boot, and may introduce the odd circumstance connected with Mr Cruncher's domestic economy, that, whereas he often came home after banking hours with clean boots, he often got up next morning to find the same boots covered with clay.

'What,' said Mr Cruncher, varying his apostrophe after missing his mark – 'what are you up to, Aggerawayter?'

'I was only saying my prayers.'

'Saying your prayers! You're a nice woman! What do you mean by flopping yourself down and praying agin me?'

'I was not praying against you; I was praying for you.'

'You weren't. And if you were, I won't be took the liberty with. Here! your mother's a nice woman, young Jerry, going a praying agin your father's prosperity. You've got a dutiful mother, you have, my son. You've got a religious mother, you have, my boy: going and flopping herself down, and praying that the bread-and-butter may be snatched out of the mouth of her only child.'

Master Cruncher (who was in his shirt) took this very ill, and, turning to his mother, strongly deprecated any praying away of his personal board.

'And what do you suppose, you conceited female,' said Mr Cruncher, with unconscious inconsistency, 'that the worth of *your* prayers may be? Name the price that you put *your* prayers at!'

'They only come from the heart, Jerry. They are worth no more than that.'

'Worth no more than that,' repeated Mr Cruncher. 'They ain't worth much, then. Whether or no, I won't be prayed agin, I tell you. I can't afford it. I'm not a going to be made unlucky by *your* sneaking. If you must go flopping yourself down, flop in favour of your husband and child, and not in opposition to 'em. If I had had any but a unnat'ral wife, and this poor boy had had any but a unnat'ral mother, I might have made some money last week instead of being counter-prayed and countermined and religiously circumwented into the worst of luck. B-u-u-ust me!' said Mr Cruncher, who all this time had been putting on his clothes, 'if I ain't, what with piety and one blowed thing and another, been choused this last week into as bad luck as ever a poor devil of a honest tradesman met with! Young Jerry, dress yourself, my boy, and while I clean my boots keep a eye upon your mother now and then, and if you see any signs of more flopping, give me a call. For, I tell you,' here he addressed his wife once more, 'I won't be gone agin, in this manner. I am as rickety as a hackney-coach, I'm as sleepy as laudanum, my lines is strained to that degree that I shouldn't know, if it wasn't for the pain in 'em, which was me and which somebody else, yet I'm none the better for it in pocket; and it's my suspicion that you've been at it from morning to night to prevent me from being the better for it in pocket, and I won't put up with it, Aggerawayter, and what do you say now!'

Growling, in addition, such phrases as 'Ah! yes! You're religious, too. You wouldn't put yourself in opposition to the interests of your husband and child, would you? Not you!' and throwing off other sarcastic sparks from the whirling grindstone of his indignation, Mr Cruncher betook himself to his boot-cleaning and his general preparation for business. In the meantime, his son, whose head was garnished with tenderer spikes, and whose young eyes stood close by one another, as his father's did, kept the required watch upon his mother. He greatly disturbed that poor woman at intervals, by darting out of his sleeping closet, where he made his toilet, with a suppressed cry of 'You are going to flop, mother. – Halloa, father!' and, after raising this fictitious alarm, darting in again with an undutiful grin.

Mr Cruncher's temper was not at all improved when he came to his breakfast. He resented Mrs Cruncher's saying grace with particular animosity.

'Now, Aggerawayter! What are you up to? At it agin?'

His wife explained that she had merely 'asked a blessing'.

'Don't do it!' said Mr Cruncher looking about, as if he rather expected to see the loaf disappear under the efficacy of his wife's petitions. 'I ain't a going to be blest out of house and home. I won't have my wittles blest off my table. Keep still!'

Exceedingly red-eyed and grim, as if he had been up all night at a party which had taken anything but a convivial turn, Jerry Cruncher worried his breakfast rather than ate it, growling over it like any four-footed inmate of a menagerie. Towards nine o'clock he smoothed his ruffled aspect, and, presenting as respectable and business-like an exterior as he could overlay his natural self with, issued forth to the occupation of the day.

A Tale of Two Cities, 1859

I'm Always Ill After Shakespeare: Books and the Theatre

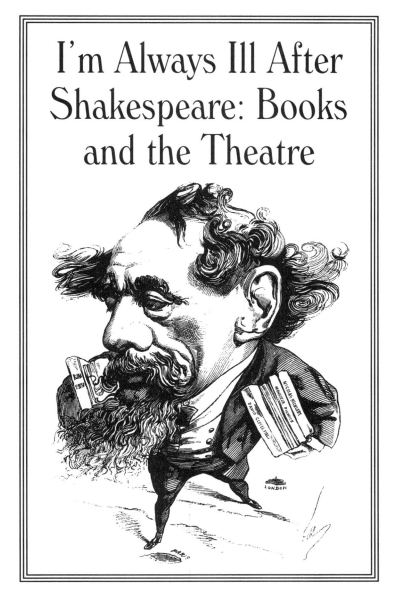

THAT DICKENS WAS A NOVELIST who could extract a certain amount of humour from any given subject is unarguable. He saw comedy everywhere and, as several of his close friends attest, his comic observations were not only confined to his novels. There are accounts of Dickens laughing uproariously through dinner parties, of him mimicking friends, relating funny stories and telling jokes, as well as being, when the mood took him, exceedingly sarcastic. For instance when George Henry Lewes (the philosopher, critic and scientist, and friend of George Eliot) wrote a series of articles entitled 'Success in Literature', Dickens responded by saying, 'Success in literature? What on earth does George Lewes know about success in literature?'

However, it *is* to his novels that we turn when we most want to experience Dickens's comic genius and it is no better expressed than when he is poking fun at his own art and those men and women who either worship or denigrate it . . .

'Poetry's unnat'ral; no man ever talked poetry 'cept a beadle on boxin' day, or Warren's blackin' or Rowland's oil, or some o' them low fellows; never you let yourself down to talk poetry, my boy.'

Mr Weller, *The Pickwick Papers*, 1836–7

Thereupon the Captain, with much alacrity, shouldered his book – for he made it a point of duty to read none but very large books on a Sunday, as having a more staid appearance: and had bargained, years ago, for a prodigious

volume at a book-stall, five lines of which utterly confounded him, insomuch that he had not yet ascertained of
what subject it treated – and withdrew.

Dombey and Son, 1846–8

'She dotes on poetry, sir. She adores it; I may say that her whole soul and mind are wound up, and entwined with it. She has produced some delightful pieces, herself, sir. You may have met with her "Ode to an Expiring Frog", sir.'

Leo Hunter, The Pickwick Papers, 1836–7

Cramped in all kinds of dim cupboards and hutches at Tellson's, the oldest of men carried on the business gravely. When they took a young man into Tellson's London house, they hid him somewhere till he was old. They kept him in a dark place, like a cheese, until he had the full Tellson flavour and blue-mould upon him. Then only was he permitted to be seen, spectacularly poring over large books and casting his breeches and gaiters into the general weight of the establishment.

A Tale of Two Cities, 1859

'. . . vether it's worth while goin' through so much, to learn so little, as the charity-boy said ven he got to the end of the alphabet, is a matter o' taste.'

Mr Weller, The Pickwick Papers, 1836–7

'. . . we have always believed a Secretary to be a piece of furniture, mostly of mahogany, lined with green baize or leather, with a lot of little drawers in it. Now, you won't think I take a liberty when I mention that you certainly ain't that.'

Mr Boffin, Our Mutual Friend, 1864–5

It was four in the afternoon – that is, the vulgar afternoon of the sun and the clock – and Mrs Wititterly reclined, according to custom, on the drawing-room sofa, while Kate read aloud a new novel in three volumes, entitled 'The Lady Flabella', which Alphonse the doubtful had procured from the library that very morning. And it was a production admirably suited to a lady labouring under Mrs Wititterly's complaint, seeing that there was not a line in it, from beginning to end, which could, by the most remote contingency, awaken the smallest excitement in any person breathing.

Nicholas Nickleby, 1838–9

❀

A.D. had no concern with anno Domini, but stood for anno Dombei – and Son.

Dombey and Son, 1846–8

❀

'"There's a lot of feet in Shakespeare's verse, but there ain't any legs worth mentioning in Shakespeare's plays, are there, Pip? Juliet, Desdemona, Lady Macbeth, and all the rest of 'em, whatever their names are, might as well have no legs at all, for anything the audience know about it, Pip . . . What's the legitimate object of the drama, Pip? Human nature. What are legs? Human nature. Then let us have plenty of leg pieces, Pip . . ."'

Mr Pip, quoting 'the Viscount',
Martin Chuzzlewit, 1843–4

'Mr Bazzard's father, being a Norfolk farmer, would have furiously laid about him with a flail, a pitch-fork, and every agricultural implement available for assaulting purposes, on the slightest hint of his son's having written a play.'

Mr Grewgious, *The Mystery of Edwin Drood*, 1870

In 1850 Dickens created a periodical called Household Words. *Its contributors (as was the wont in those days) were to remain anonymous, but there were several writers who began to rebel against this ignominy, seeing it as an injustice.*

'But,' said Dickens, 'the periodical is anonymous throughout.'

'Yes,' said his friend, Douglas Jerrold, while reading the words that appeared at the top of every single page, '"Conducted by Charles Dickens." I see it is – *mon*onymous throughout.'

From *Charles Dickens: His Tragedy and Triumph*,
EDGAR JOHNSON, 1977

'I'm always ill after Shakespeare.'
Mrs Wititterly, *Nicholas Nickleby*, 1838–9

'. . . a literary man – *with* a wooden leg – is always liable to jealousy.'

Mr Boffin, *Our Mutual Friend*, 1864–5

'Well, sir,' returned Mr Tapley, 'sooner than you should do that, I'll com-ply. It's a considerable invasion of a man's jollity to be made so partickler welcome, but a Werb is a word as signifies to be, to do, or to suffer (which is all the grammar, and enough too, as ever I wos taught); and if there's a Werb alive, I'm it. For I'm always a-bein', sometimes a-doin', and continually a-sufferin'.'

Martin Chuzzlewit, 1843–4

No one who can read, ever looks at a book, even unopened on a shelf, like one who cannot.

Our Mutual Friend, 1864–5

'. . . there are books of which the backs and covers are by far the best parts.'

Mr Brownlow, *Oliver Twist*, 1837–9

Tired of working, and conversing with Miss Twinkleton, she suggested working and reading: to which Miss Twinkleton readily assented, as an admirable reader, of tried powers. But Rosa soon made the discovery that Miss Twinkleton didn't read fairly. She cut the love-scenes, interpolated passages in praise of female celibacy, and was guilty of other glaring pious frauds.

The Mystery of Edwin Drood, 1870

A Descriptive
Advertisement

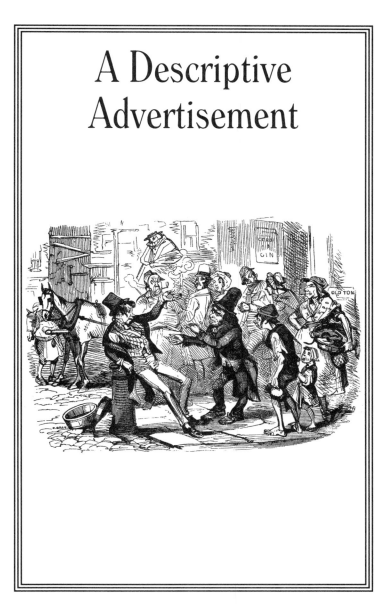

The Old Curiosity Shop is one of Dickens's darkest, most bleak novels. Half fairy tale, half grim reality, it is the story of Little Nell and her persecution by the odious dwarf, Quilp. That there is little humour in the novel is hardly surprising although Oscar Wilde (towards the end of the century) is said to have remarked that one must have a heart of stone to read the account of Little Nell's death without laughing. Of course, that was not the desired effect and the death of Little Nell resulted in a whole nation of readers mourning her passing. Thomas Carlyle, not one of Dickens's greatest supporters, was said to be grief-stricken. Lord Jeffrey, the literary critic of *The Edinburgh Review*, was found in tears and, most extraordinary of all, crowds of people gathered at the docks in New York and shouted to an incoming vessel, 'Is Little Nell dead?'

But it is without a doubt Quilp, not Little Nell, who stands at the centre of this novel and who is Dickens's most compelling and memorable creation. Deformed, with a gigantic head and dwarfish body, he is at once both

repulsive and fascinating. That Dickens could conceive such a monster and then extract humour from his odious creation must surely be testimony to his genius.

The bedroom-door on the staircase being unlocked, Mr Quilp slipped in, and planted himself behind the door of communication between that chamber and the sitting-room, which standing ajar to render both more airy, and having a very convenient chink (of which he had often availed himself for purposes of espial, and had indeed enlarged with his pocket-knife), enabled him not only to hear, but to see distinctly, what was passing.

Applying his eye to this convenient place, he descried Mr Brass seated at the table with pen, ink, and paper, and the case-bottle of rum – his own case-bottle, and his own particular Jamaica – convenient to his hand; with hot water, fragrant lemons, white lump sugar, and all things fitting; from which choice materials, Sampson, by no means insensible to their claims upon his attention, had compounded a mighty glass of punch reeking hot; which he was at that very moment stirring up with a teaspoon, and contemplating with looks in which a faint assumption of sentimental regret, struggled but weakly with a bland and comfortable joy. At the same table, with both her elbows upon it, was Mrs Jiniwin; no longer sipping other people's punch feloniously with teaspoons, but taking deep draughts from a jorum of her own; while her daughter – not exactly with ashes on her head, or sackcloth on her back, but preserving a very decent and becoming appearance of sorrow nevertheless – was reclining in an easy chair, and soothing her grief with a smaller allowance of the same glib liquid. There were also present, a couple of water-side men, bearing between them certain machines called drags; even these fellows were accommodated with a stiff glass a-piece; and as they drank with a great relish, and were naturally of a red-nosed, pimple-faced, convivial look, their presence rather increased than detracted from that decided appearance of comfort, which was the great characteristic of the party.

'If I could poison that dear old lady's rum and water,' murmured Quilp, 'I'd die happy.'

'Ah!' said Mr Brass, breaking the silence, and raising his eyes to the ceiling with a sigh, 'Who knows but he may be looking down upon us now! Who knows but he may be surveying of us from – from somewheres or another, and contemplating us with a watchful eye! Oh Lor!'

Here Mr Brass stopped to drink half his punch, and then resumed; looking at the other half, as he spoke, with a dejected smile.

'I can almost fancy,' said the lawyer shaking his head, 'that I see his eye glistening down at the very bottom of my liquor. When shall we look upon his like again? Never, never! One minute we are here' – holding his tumbler before his eyes – 'the next we are there' – gulping down its contents, and striking himself emphatically a little below the chest – 'in the silent tomb. To think that I should be drinking his very rum! It seems like a dream.'

With the view, no doubt, of testing the reality of his position, Mr Brass pushed his tumbler as he spoke towards Mrs Jiniwin for the purpose of being replenished; and turned towards the attendant mariners.

'The search has been quite unsuccessful then?'

'Quite, master. But I should say that if he turns up anywhere, he'll come ashore somewhere about Grinidge to-morrow, at ebb tide, eh, mate?'

The other gentleman assented, observing that he was expected at the Hospital, and that several pensioners would be ready to receive him whenever he arrived.

'Then we have nothing for it but resignation,' said Mr Brass; 'nothing but resignation and expectation. It would be a comfort to have his body; it would be a dreary comfort.'

'Oh, beyond a doubt,' assented Mrs Jiniwin hastily; 'if we once had that, we should be quite sure.'

'With regard to the descriptive advertisement,' said Sampson Brass, taking up his pen. 'It is a melancholy pleasure to recall his traits. Respecting his legs now –?'

'Crooked, certainly,' said Mrs Jiniwin.

'Do you think they *were* crooked?' said Brass, in an insinuating tone. 'I think I see them now coming up the street very wide apart, in nankeen' pantaloons a little shrunk and without straps. Ah! what a vale of tears we live in. Do we say crooked?'

'I think they were a little so,' observed Mrs Quilp with a sob.

'Legs crooked,' said Brass, writing as he spoke. 'Large head, short body, legs crooked –'

'Very crooked,' suggested Mrs Jiniwin.

'We'll not say very crooked, ma'am,' said Brass piously. 'Let us not bear hard upon the weaknesses of the deceased. He is gone, ma'am, to where his legs will never come in question. – We will content ourselves with crooked, Mrs Jiniwin.'

'I thought you wanted the truth,' said the old lady. 'That's all.'

'Bless your eyes, how I love you,' muttered Quilp. 'There she goes again. Nothing but punch!'

'This is an occupation,' said the lawyer, laying down his pen and emptying his glass, 'which seems to bring him before my eyes like the Ghost of Hamlet's father, in the very clothes that he wore on work-a-days. His coat, his waistcoat, his shoes and stockings, his trousers, his hat, his wit and humour, his pathos and his umbrella, all come before me like visions of my youth. His linen!' said Mr Brass smiling fondly at the wall, 'his linen which was always of a particular colour, for such was his whim and fancy – how plain I see his linen now!'

'You had better go on, sir,' said Mrs Jiniwin impatiently.

'True, ma'am, true,' cried Mr Brass. 'Our faculties must not freeze with grief. I'll trouble you for a little more of that, ma'am. A question now arises, with relation to his nose.'

'Flat,' said Mrs Jiniwin.

'Aquiline!' cried Quilp, thrusting in his head, and striking the feature with his fist. 'Aquiline, you hag. Do you see it? Do you call this flat? Do you? Eh?'

'Oh capital, capital!' shouted Brass, from the mere force of habit. 'Excellent! How very good he is! He's a most remarkable man – so extremely whimsical! Such an amazing power of taking people by surprise!'

Quilp paid no regard whatever to these compliments, nor to the dubious and frightened look into which the lawyer gradually subsided, nor to the shrieks of his wife and mother-in-law, nor to the latter's running from the room, nor to the former's fainting away. Keeping his eye fixed on Sampson Brass, he walked up to the table, and beginning with his glass, drank off the contents, and went regularly round until he had emptied the other two, when he seized the case-bottle, and hugging it under his arm, surveyed him with a most extraordinary leer.

'Not yet, Sampson,' said Quilp. 'Not just yet!'

'Oh very good indeed!' cried Brass, recovering his spirits a little. 'Ha ha ha! Oh exceedingly good! There's not another man alive who could carry it off like that. A most difficult position to carry off. But he has such a flow of good-humour, such an amazing flow!'

'Good night,' said the dwarf, nodding expressively.

'Good night, sir, good night,' cried the lawyer, retreating backwards towards the door. 'This is a joyful occasion indeed, extremely joyful. Ha ha ha! oh very rich, very rich indeed, remarkably so!'

The Old Curiosity Shop, 1840–1

Please, Sir . . .
I Want Some More

George Cruikshank

IN AN AGE when half the population were either starving to death or fed on such delicacies as gruel, it is hardly surprising that many of Dickens's novels use food as a means of highlighting social iniquity. Of course the scene in *Oliver Twist* where Oliver 'asks for more' is now etched into the collective consciousness, but there are several other scenes in Dickens's novels that combine both humour and pathos where food is concerned – in *David Copperfield*, for instance, where the naïve young boy is cheated out of his meal by a very unscrupulous waiter.

'Please, sir,' replied Oliver, 'I want some more.'

The master aimed a blow at Oliver's head with the ladle; pinioned him in his arms; and shrieked aloud for the beadle.

The board were sitting in solemn conclave, when Mr Bumble rushed into the room in great excitement, and addressing the gentleman in the high chair, said, 'Mr Limbkins, I beg your pardon, sir! Oliver Twist has asked for more!'

There was a general start. Horror was depicted on every countenance.

'For *more*!' said Mr Limbkins. 'Compose yourself, Bumble, and answer me distinctly. Do I understand that he asked for more, after he had eaten the supper allotted by the dietary?'

'He did, sir,' replied Bumble.

'That boy will be hung,' said the gentleman in the white waistcoat. 'I know that boy will be hung.'

Oliver Twist, 1837–9

Mr Pecksniff promptly departed, followed by Mrs Gamp, who, seeing that he took a bottle and glass from the cupboard, and carried it in his hand, was much softened.

Martin Chuzzlewit, 1843–4

❁

'Tongue; well, that's a wery good thing when it ain't a woman's.'

Mr Weller, *The Pickwick Papers*, 1836–7

❁

'Tell Mrs Gamp to come up-stairs,' said Mould. 'Now Mrs Gamp, what's *your* news?'

The lady in question was by this time in the doorway, curtseying to Mrs Mould. At the same moment a peculiar fragrance was borne upon the breeze, as if a passing fairy had hiccoughed, and had previously been to a wine-vault.

Martin Chuzzlewit, 1843–4

❁

'It's not Madness, ma'am,' replied Mr Bumble, after a few moments of deep meditation. 'It's Meat.'

'What?' exclaimed Mrs Sowerberry.

'Meat, ma'am, meat,' replied Bumble, with stern emphasis. 'You've over-fed him . . . If you had kept the boy on gruel, ma'am, this would never have happened.'

'Dear, dear!' ejaculated Mrs Sowerberry, piously raising her eyes to the kitchen ceiling: 'this comes of being liberal!'

Oliver Twist, 1837–9

'There's half a pint of ale for you. Will you have it now?'

I thanked him and said, 'Yes.' Upon which he poured it out of a jug into a large tumbler, and held it up against the light, and made it look beautiful.

'My eye!' he said. 'It seems a good deal, don't it?'

'It does seem a good deal,' I answered with a smile. For it was quite delightful to me, to find him so pleasant. He was a twinkling-eyed, pimple-faced man, with his hair standing upright all over his head; and as he stood with one arm a-kimbo, holding up the glass to the light with the other hand, he looked quite friendly.

'There was a gentleman here, yesterday,' he said – 'a stout gentleman, by the name of Topsawyer – perhaps you know him?'

'No,' I said, 'I don't think – '

'In breeches and gaiters, broad-brimmed hat, grey coat, speckled choker,' said the waiter.

'No,' I said bashfully, 'I haven't the pleasure – '

'He came in here,' said the waiter, looking at the light through the tumbler, 'ordered a glass of this ale – *would* order it – I told him not – drank it, and fell dead. It was too old for him. It oughtn't to be drawn; that's the fact.'

I was very much shocked to hear of this melancholy accident, and said I thought I had better have some water.

'Why, you see,' said the waiter, still looking at the light through the tumbler, with one of his eyes shut up, 'our people don't like things being ordered and left. It offends 'em. But *I*'ll drink it, if you like. I'm used to it, and use is everything. I don't think it'll hurt me, if I throw my head back, and take it off quick. Shall I?'

I replied that he would much oblige me by drinking it, if he thought he could do it safely, but by no means other-wise. When he did throw his head back, and take it off quick, I had a horrible fear, I confess, of seeing him meet the fate of the lamented Mr Topsawyer, and fall lifeless on the carpet. But it didn't hurt him. On the contrary, I thought he seemed the fresher for it.

'What have we got here?' he said, putting a fork into my dish. 'Not chops?'

'Chops,' I said.

'Lord bless my soul!' he exclaimed, 'I didn't know they were chops. Why, a chop's the very thing to take off the bad effects of that beer! Ain't it lucky?'

So he took a chop by the bone in one hand, and a potato in the other, and ate away with a very good appetite, to my extreme satisfaction. He afterwards took another chop, and another potato; and after that, another chop and another potato. When we had done, he brought me a pudding, and having set it before me, seemed to ruminate, and to become absent in his mind for some moments.

'How's the pie?' he said, rousing himself.

'It's a pudding,' I made answer.

'Pudding!' he exclaimed. 'Why, bless me, so it is! What!' looking at it nearer. 'You don't mean to say it's a batter-pudding!'

'Yes, it is indeed.'

'Why, a batter-pudding,' he said, taking up a table-spoon, 'is my favourite pudding! Ain't that lucky? Come on, little 'un, and let's see who'll get most.'

The waiter certainly got most. He entreated me more than once to come in and win, but what with his table-spoon to my tea-spoon, his dispatch to my dispatch, and his appetite to my appetite, I was left far behind at the first mouthful, and had no chance with him. I never saw anyone enjoy a pudding so much, I think; and he laughed, when it was all gone, as if his enjoyment of it lasted still.

Finding him so very friendly and companionable, it was then that I asked for the pen and ink and paper, to write to Peggotty. He not only brought it immediately, but was good enough to look over me while I wrote the letter. When I had finished it, he asked me where I was going to school.

I said, 'Near London,' which was all I knew.

'Oh, my eye!' he said, looking very low-spirited, 'I am sorry for that.'

'Why?' I asked him.

'Oh, Lord!' he said, shaking his head, 'that's the school where they broke the boy's ribs – two ribs – a little boy he was. I should say he was – let me see – how old are you, about?'

I told him between eight and nine.

'That's just his age,' he said. 'He was eight years and six months old when they broke his first rib; eight years and eight months old when they broke his second, and did for him.'

I could not disguise from myself, or from the waiter, that this was an uncomfortable coincidence, and inquired how it was done. His answer was not cheering to my spirits, for it consisted of two dismal words, 'With whopping.'

The blowing of the coach-horn in the yard was a seasonable diversion, which made me get up and hesitatingly inquire, in the mingled pride and diffidence of having a purse (which I took out of my pocket), if there were anything to pay.

'There's a sheet of letter-paper,' he returned. 'Did you ever buy a sheet of letter-paper?'

I could not remember that I ever had.

'It's dear,' he said, 'on account of the duty. Threepence. That's the way we're taxed in this country. There's nothing else, except the waiter. Never mind the ink. *I* lose by that.'

'What should you – what should I – how much ought I

to – what would it be right to pay the waiter, if you please?' I stammered, blushing.

'If I hadn't a family, and that family hadn't the cow-pock,' said the waiter, 'I wouldn't take a sixpence. If I didn't support a aged pairint, and a lovely sister,' – here the waiter was greatly agitated – 'I wouldn't take a farthing. If I had a good place, and was treated well here, I should beg acceptance of a trifle, instead of taking of it. But I live on broken wittles – and I sleep on the coals' – here the waiter burst into tears.

I was very much concerned for his misfortunes, and felt that any recognition short of ninepence would be mere brutality and hardness of heart. Therefore I gave him one of my three bright shillings, which he received with much humility and veneration, and spun up with his thumb, directly afterwards, to try the goodness of.

It was a little disconcerting to me to find, when I was being helped up behind the coach, that I was supposed to have eaten all the dinner without any assistance. I discovered this, from overhearing the lady in the bow-window say to the guard, 'Take care of that child, George, or he'll burst!' and from observing that the women-servants who were about the place came out to look and giggle at me as a young phenomenon. My unfortunate friend the waiter, who had quite recovered his spirits, did not appear to be disturbed by this, but joined in the general admiration without being at all confused. If I had any doubt of him, I suppose this half awakened it; but I am inclined to believe that with the simple confidence of a child, and the natural reliance of a child upon superior years (qualities I am very sorry any children should prematurely change for worldly wisdom), I had no serious mistrust of him on the whole, even then.

David, *David Copperfield*, 1849–50

Podsnappery

Within the illustration:
SIGNOR
BILL SMETHI'S
GRAND
BALL
will take place
on
The First of July
in the garden

George Cruikshank

With the exception of *The Mystery of Edwin Drood*, which sadly remained unfinished at the time of Dickens's death, *Our Mutual Friend* was the last of Dickens's novels. Lighter in tone than either *Great Expectations* or *A Tale of Two Cities* (its two immediate predecessors), *Our Mutual Friend* contains all one expects from Dickens's work and in particular some wonderful characters, among them the one-legged Silas Wegg, Jenny Wren who makes dresses for dolls and last, but not least, the pompous upholder of all things conventional, Mr Podsnap. Podsnap is in fact a prime example of all the things that Dickens found loathsome in a man; he is a philistine and xenophobe, he turns his back on anything that doesn't fit his picture of society . . . in fact Podsnappery is, as Edgar Johnson put it in his marvellous biography of Dickens, 'the dominant attitude of respectable society, a vast, meretricious, and vulgar materialism'.

Mr Podsnap was well-to-do, and stood very high in Mr Podsnap's opinion.

Hideous solidity was the characteristic of the Podsnap plate. Everything was made to look as heavy as it could, and to take up as much room as possible. Everything said boastfully, 'Here you have as much of me in my ugliness as if I were only lead; but I am so many ounces of precious metal, worth so much an ounce; – wouldn't you like to melt me down?' . . . The majority of the guests were like the plate, and included several heavy articles weighing ever so much.

Mr Podsnap's world was not a very large world, morally; no, nor even geographically: seeing that, although his business was sustained upon commerce with other countries, he considered other countries, with that important reservation, a mistake, and of their manners and customs would conclusively observe, 'Not English!' . . .

The Podsnaps lived in a shady angle adjoining Portman Square. They were a kind of people certain to dwell in the shade, wherever they dwelt.

'There is not,' said Mr Podsnap, flushing angrily, 'there is not a country in the world, sir, where so noble a provision is made for the poor as in this country.'

The meek man was quite willing to concede that, but perhaps it rendered the matter even worse, as showing that there must be something appallingly wrong somewhere.

'Where?' said Mr Podsnap.

The meek man hinted, Wouldn't it be well to try, very seriously, to find out where?

'Ah!' said Mr Podsnap. 'Easy to say somewhere; not so easy to say where! But I see what you are driving at. I knew it from the first. Centralization. No. Never with my consent. Not English.'

As a so eminently respectable man, Mr Podsnap was sensible of its being required of him to take Providence under his protection. Consequently, he always knew exactly what Providence meant. Inferior and less respectable men might fall short of that mark, but Mr Podsnap was always up to it. And it was very remarkable (and must have been very comfortable) that what Providence meant was invariably what Mr Podsnap meant.

❖

Veneering . . . finds Podsnap reading the paper, standing, and inclined to be oratorical over the astonishing discovery he has made, that Italy is not England.

The foreign gentleman found it, without doubt, énormément riche.

'Enormously Rich, We say,' returned Mr Podsnap, in a condescending manner. 'Our English adverbs do Not terminate in Mong, and We Pronounce the "ch" as if there were a "t" before it. We say Ritch.'

'Reetch,' remarked the foreign gentleman.

'And Do You Find, Sir,' pursued Mr Podsnap, with dignity, 'Many Evidences that Strike You of our British Constitution in the Streets Of The World's Metropolis, London, Londres, London?'

The foreign gentleman begged to be pardoned, but did not altogether understand.

'The Constitution Britannique,' Mr Podsnap explained, as if he were teaching in an infant school. 'We Say British, But You Say Britannique, You Know' (forgivingly, as if that were not his fault). 'The Constitution, Sir.'

Our Mutual Friend, 1864–5

Papa, Potatoes, Poultry, Prunes and Prism: Nonsenses

NOTICE
THE
GAMEKEEPER
HAS ORDERS
TO SHOOT ALL
DOGS
FOUND IN
THIS
INCLOSURE

THAT THERE ARE SO MANY humorous moments in Dickens's novels makes it well-nigh impossible to include each and every one – however, below are a few of the choicest moments . . .

———————◆◆◆◆———————

'Heads, heads – take care of your heads!' cried the loquacious stranger, as they came out under the low archway, which in those days formed the entrance to the coachyard. 'Terrible place – dangerous work – other day – five children – mother – tall lady, eating sandwiches – forgot the arch – crash – knock – children look round – mother's head off – sandwich in her hand – no mouth to put it in – head of a family off – shocking, shocking!'

The Pickwick Papers, 1836–7

✤

'Do you know, now,' said Mr Pecksniff, folding his hands, and looking at his young relation with an air of pensive interest, 'that I should very much like to see your notion of a cowhouse?'

But Martin by no means appeared to relish this suggestion.

'A pump,' said Mr Pecksniff, 'is a very chaste practice. I have found that a lamp-post is calculated to refine the mind and give it a classical tendency. An ornamental turnpike has a remarkable effect upon the imagination. What do you say to beginning with an ornamental turnpike?'

Martin Chuzzlewit, 1843–4

'I am sure there was a case in the day before yesterday's paper, extracted from one of the French newspapers, about a journeyman shoemaker who was jealous of a young girl in an adjoining village, because she wouldn't shut herself up in an airtight three-pair of stairs, and charcoal herself to death with him; and who went and hid himself in a wood with a sharp-pointed knife, and rushed out, as she was passing by with a few friends, and killed himself first, and then all the friends, and then her – no, killed all the friends first, and then herself and then *himself* – which it is quite frightful to think of. Somehow or other,' added Mrs Nickleby, after a momentary pause, 'they always *are* journeyman shoemakers who do these things in France, according to the papers. I don't know how it is – something in the leather, I suppose.'

Mrs Nickleby, *Nicholas Nickleby*, 1838–9

'Something will come of this. I hope it mayn't be human gore!'

Simon Tappertit, *Barnaby Rudge*, 1841,
on grinding up tools

'. . . Take another glass of wine, and excuse my mentioning that society as a body does not expect one to be so strictly conscientious in emptying one's glass, as to turn it bottom upwards with the rim on one's nose.'

Herbert Pocket, *Great Expectations*, 1860-1

When you have parted with a man, at two o'clock in the morning, on terms of the utmost good fellowship, and he meets you again, at half-past nine, and greets you as a serpent, it is not unreasonable to conclude that something of an unpleasant nature has occurred meanwhile.

The Pickwick Papers, 1836–7

'There are only two styles of portrait painting; the serious and the smirk.'

Miss La Creevy, *Nicholas Nickleby*, 1838–9

*As Peter Ackroyd points out in his wonderful biography of
Charles Dickens, the following letter from Fanny Squeers
is often described as the funniest letter in the English lan-
guage excepting 'De Profundis' by Oscar Wilde.*

Dotheboys Hall,
Thursday Morning

Sir, My pa requests me to write to you. The doctors consider it doubtful whether he will ever recuvver the use of
his legs which prevents his holding a pen.

   We are in a state of mind byond everything, and my pa
is one mask of brooses both blue and green likewise two
forms are steepled in his Goar. We were kimpelled to have
him carried down into the kitchen where he now lays. You
will judge from this that he has been brought very low.

   When your nevew that you recommended for a teacher
had done this to my pa and jumped upon his body with
his feet and also langwedge which I will not pollewt my
pen with describing, he assaulted my ma with dreadful
violence, dashed her to the earth, and drove her back
comb several inches into her head. A very little more and
it must have entered her skull. We have a medical
certifiket that if it had, the tortershell would have affected
the brain . . .

   I remain
   Yours and cetrer
   FANNY SQUEERS
   P.S. I pity his ignorance and despise him.

Nicholas Nickleby, 1838–9

'Papa, potatoes, poultry, prunes and prism, are all very good words for the lips; especially prunes and prism.'
Mrs General, *Little Dorrit*, 1855–7

'It's over, and can't be helped, and that's one consolation, as they always says in Turkey, ven they cuts the wrong man's head off.'
Sam Weller, *The Pickwick Papers*, 1836–7

The one great principle of the English law is to make business for itself.
Bleak House, 1852-3

. . . Mr and Mrs Boffin sat staring at mid-air, and Mrs Wilfer sat silently giving them to understand that every breath she drew required to be drawn with a self-denial rarely paralleled in history . . .
Our Mutual Friend, 1864–5

I never had anything left to me but relations.
Observation of Charles Dickens following the death of his brother, Alfred, whose family Charles was left to look after, 1860

'Ah! you should keep dogs – fine animals – sagacious creatures – dog of my own once – Pointer – surprising instinct
– out shooting one day – entering inclosure – whistled –
dog stopped – whistled again – Ponto – no go; stock still –
called him – Ponto, Ponto – wouldn't move – dog
transfixed – staring at a board – looked up, saw an
inscription – "Gamekeeper has orders to shoot all dogs
found in this inclosure" – wouldn't pass it – wonderful
dog – valuable dog that – very.'

'The stranger' (Mr Jingle), *The Pickwick Papers*,
1836–7

🌼

'Here's the rule for bargains: "Do other men, for they
would do you." That's the true business precept. All others are counterfeits.'

Jonas Chuzzlewit, *Martin Chuzzlewit*, 1843–4

🌼

'There can be no doubt,' said Mrs Nickleby, 'that he *is* a
gentleman, and has the manners of a gentleman, and the
appearance of a gentleman, although he does wear smalls
and grey worsted stockings. That may be eccentricity, or
he may be proud of his legs. I don't see why he shouldn't
be. The Prince Regent was proud of his legs, and so was
Daniel Lambert, who was also a fat man; *he* was proud of
his legs. So was Miss Biffin: she was – no,' added Mrs
Nickleby, correcting herself, 'I think she had only toes, but
the principle is the same.'

Nicholas Nickleby, 1838–9

There were three other Young Barnacles, from three other offices, insipid to all the senses, and terribly in want of seasoning, doing the marriage as they would have 'done' the Nile, Old Rome . . . or Jerusalem.

Little Dorrit, 1855–7

✾

'Many and many is the circuit this pony has gone,' said Mr Crummles, flicking him skilfully on the eyelid for old acquaintance' sake. 'He is quite one of us. His mother was on the stage.'

'Was she, indeed?' rejoined Nicholas.

'She ate apple-pie at a circus for upwards of fourteen years,' said the manager; 'fired pistols, and went to bed in a nightcap; and, in short, took the low comedy entirely. His father was a dancer.'

'Was he at all distinguished?'

'Not very,' said the manager. 'He was rather a low sort of pony. The fact is, he had been originally jobbed out by the day, and he never quite got over his old habits. He was clever in melodrama too, but too broad – too broad. When the mother died, he took the port-wine business.'

'The port-wine business!' cried Nicholas.

'Drinking port-wine with the clown,' said the manager; 'but he was greedy, and one night bit off the bowl of the glass, and choked himself, so that his vulgarity was the death of him at last.'

Nicholas Nickleby, 1838–9

... Mrs Gamp took him by the collar of his coat, and gave some dozen or two of hearty shakes backward and forward in his chair; that exercise being considered by the disciples of the Prig school of nursing (who are very numerous among professional ladies) as exceedingly conducive to repose, and highly beneficial to the performance of nervous functions. Its effect in this instance was to render the patient so giddy and addle-headed, that he could say nothing more; which Mrs Gamp regarded as the triumph of her art.

'There!' she said, loosening the old man's cravat, in consequence of his being rather black in the face, after this scientific treatment. 'Now, I hope, you're easy in your mind. If you should turn at all faint we can soon revive you, sir, I promige you. Bite a person's thumbs, or turn their fingers the wrong way,' said Mrs Gamp, smiling with the consciousness of at once imparting pleasure and instruction to her auditors, 'and they comes to, wonderful, Lord bless you!'

Martin Chuzzlewit, 1843–4

'Hackney coaches, my lord, are such nasty things, that it's almost better to walk at any time, for although I believe a hackney coachman can be transported for life, if he has a broken window, still they are so reckless, that they nearly all have broken windows. I once had a swelled face for six weeks, my lord, from riding in a hackney coach – I think it was a hackney coach,' said Mrs Nickleby reflecting, 'though I'm not quite certain whether it wasn't a chariot; at all events I know it was dark green, with a very long number, beginning with a nought and ending with a nine – no, beginning with a nine, and ending with a nought, that was it, and of course the stamp office people would know at once whether it was a coach or a chariot if any inquiries were made there – however that was, there it was with a broken window and there was I for six weeks with a swelled face . . .'.

Nicholas Nickleby, 1838–9

It is one of the easiest achievements in life to offend your family when your family want to get rid of you.

Our Mutual Friend, 1864–5

'. . . Your grandmother, Kate, was exactly the same – precisely. The least excitement, the slightest surprise, she fainted away directly. I have heard her say, often and often, that when she was a young lady, and before she was married, she was turning a corner into Oxford Street one day, when she ran against her own hairdresser, who, it seems, was escaping from a bear; – the mere suddenness of the encounter made her faint away directly. Wait, though,' added Mrs Nickleby, pausing to consider. 'Let me be sure I'm right. Was it her hairdresser who had escaped from a bear, or was it a bear who had escaped from her hairdresser's? I declare I can't remember just now, but the hairdresser was a very handsome man, I know, and quite a gentleman in his manners; so that it has nothing to do with the point of the story.'

Nicholas Nickleby, 1838–9

... still his philanthropy was of that gunpowderous sort that the difference between it and animosity was hard to determine.

The Mystery of Edwin Drood, 1870,
of Mr Honeythunder

Reginald Wilfer is a name with rather a grand sound, suggesting on first acquaintance, brasses in country churches, scrolls in stained-glass windows, and generally the De Wilfers who came over with the Conqueror. For, it is a remarkable fact in genealogy that no De Anyones ever came over with Anybody else.

Our Mutual Friend, 1864–5

'There is no such passion in human nature, as the passion for gravy among commercial gentlemen.'

Mrs Todgers, *Martin Chuzzlewit*, 1843–4

'Dead!' replied the other, with a contemptuous emphasis. 'Not he. You won't catch Ned a-dying easy. No, no. He knows better than that.'

Bill Simmons, *Martin Chuzzlewit*, 1843–4

DATE DUE